Economics in the
Public Service

Contributors

James Tobin
Paul A. Samuelson
Robert M. Solow
Franco Modigliani
Richard N. Cooper
Anne O. Krueger
Lloyd Ulman
Joseph A. Pechman
Richard A. Musgrave
Gardner Ackley
Walter W. Heller

Economics in the Public Service

Papers in Honor of Walter W. Heller

EDITED BY JOSEPH A. PECHMAN AND N. J. SIMLER

W. W. NORTON & COMPANY
NEW YORK   LONDON

W. W. Norton & Company, Inc.
500 Fifth Avenue
New York, N.Y. 10110

W. W. Norton & Company Ltd.
37 Great Russell Street
London WC1B 3NU

ISBN 0 393 01512 2

1 2 3 4 5 6 7 8 9 0

Contents

Preface

This small volume marks a large event: the celebration of the sixty-fifth birthday of our distinguished colleague, Walter W. Heller. The papers and the comments that follow them were presented at a two-day Conference on Economic Policy in Minneapolis in September 1980, which was attended by some seventy of Walter Heller's friends and associates.

The conference was organized and brought to fruition by John H. Kareken of the University of Minnesota, with the assistance of Joseph A. Pechman of the Brookings Institution and N. J. Simler of the University of Minnesota and the cooperation of Emily ("Johnny") Heller. The Federal Reserve Bank of Minneapolis kindly made available its conference facilities, and a number of donors generously provided the necessary funding (see page 253).

Walter Heller's professional career spans four decades, and most readers of this volume are familiar with its salient aspects. He is best known for his service as chairman of the Council of Economic Advisers in 1961–64, a period of economic growth and price stability unparalleled in recent U.S. history. Since then, he has served as president of the American Economic Association and has been a leading figure in professional and public discussions of economic problems and policies.

What may not be as well known as Walter Heller's published works or his contributions in the public service is his high regard for, and his long devotion to, teaching economics. He has been a member of the University of Minnesota faculty for thirty-five years and a Regents' Professor for the last fifteen, teaching macroeconomics, public finance, and public policy. Since 1964 the introductory course in macroeconomics has been structured around his weekly lectures. The course has prospered and, in recent times, he has each year introduced more than twenty-five hundred undergraduates to the world of economics. For over a decade he has conducted a graduate seminar on the public economy, the continuing aim of which has been to examine the nature, purpose, and effects of the role of government in economic activity.

The contributors to this volume all served as members, staff economists, or consultants of Walter Heller's Council of Economic Advisers. The papers cover the whole range of issues which were of major concern at that time and which still hold the attention of economists, policymakers, and the public alike. They are presented in this volume to advance public understanding of the nation's difficult economic problems and as a tribute to the most effective economic practitioner of our generation.

Joseph A. Pechman
N. J. Simler

November 1981

Economics in the
Public Service

Steering the Economy Then and Now

James Tobin

As chairman of the Council of Economic Advisers throughout the first Kennedy-Johnson administration, 1961-64, Walter Heller established the "New Economics" as the reigning orthodoxy of macroeconomic policy in Washington and in the country at large. The theory can be summarized in two propositions: 1) Governmental management of aggregate demand is necessary not only to diminish wasteful fluctuations in economic activity but also to attain desirable levels and trends in real economic performance. Compensatory demand management can and should be used to damp business cycles, but stabilization per se is not desirable if it leaves the economy chronically below the track of potential output corresponding to full utilization of its resources. 2) Demand management requires the active use of both fiscal and monetary instruments.

Today these propositions are no longer fashionable. Active demand management is ridiculed as "fine tuning," a casual hyperbolic phrase of Walter's, reminding us that his exuberant and inventive knack for metaphors sometimes backfired. The notion that macroeconomic policy should aim at *real* targets—employment, output, growth— is challenged by renascent faith that a market economy will find on its own the optimal values of real variables. The idea that fiscal instruments play an important role in macroeconomic stabilization is submerged in a monetarist tide.

Having defended the true faith on several other occasions,[1] I shall limit repetition here. In Part I, I shall discuss Heller's emphasis on fiscal policy as a tool of stabilization. In Part II, I shall review the strategy and success of the Heller scenario for 1961-65. Finally, in Part III, I shall speculate on the possibility and the requisite ingredients for a similar scenario 1981-85.

I. Fiscal Policy as an Instrument of Demand Management

The monetarist critique of fiscal policy was chronologically the first major attack on Heller's "New Economics," and I shall begin by reexamining Heller's "fiscalism." I suppose that if any American economist after Alvin Hansen and Leon Keyserling deserved the label "fiscalist," it was Walter Heller. However, I always thought that to describe the controversy of the 1960s as monetarism vs. fiscalism was a tendentious travesty. I believe the original sin was David Fand's.[2] The labels were irresistible in the press; journalists love simplistic dramatic dichotomies. The facts, of course, were not symmetrical. While the monetarists dismissed fiscal measures, the so-called "New Economists," including Heller, regarded monetary instruments as effective and important for good or ill and

1. J. Tobin, *The New Economics One Decade Older* (Princeton: Princeton University Press, 1974).
—"How Dead is Keynes?" *Economic Inquiry*, vol. XV, no. 4, October 1977, pp. 459-68.
—*Asset Accumulation and Economic Activity: Reflections on Contemporary Macroeconomic Theory*, Yrjo Jahnsson Lectures (Oxford: Basil Blackwell, 1980).
—"Stabilization Policy Ten Years After," *Brookings Papers on Economic Activity*, vol. 1, 1980, pp. 19-72.
—"The Monetarist Counter-Revolution Today—An Appraisal," *Economic Journal*, forthcoming issue, 1981.
2. D. Fand, "Monetarism and Fiscalism," *Banca Nazionale del Lavoro Quarterly Review*, September 1970, pp. 3-34.

worried about the proper mix of monetary and fiscal measures.

I propose to review the series of theoretical arguments advanced against the macroeconomic efficacy of fiscal policies.

1. *Inelasticity of demand for money* with respect to interest rates has long been recognized as a case in which fiscal policy—or any other exogenous "IS" shift unaccompanied by a compensating shift in excess demand for money—would be powerless to alter aggregate real demand at existing prices. In the Hicksian "IS–LM" framework this inelasticity appeared to be not only a sufficient but also—with an exception noted below in item 2—a necessary condition for the proposition. Otherwise an IS shock, such as delivered by fiscal expansion or contraction, would alter the income velocity of an unchanged money stock, generally by interest rate changes that induce greater or lesser economy in cash management. Systematic, endogenous, procyclical variation of velocity did not depend on "liquidity trap" conditions, which Keynes himself and postwar Keynesians regarded as abnormal and unusual, characteristic only of severe depression. Consequently, it was puzzling when monetarists appeared to regard the absence of those conditions as sufficient refutation of Keynesian conclusions about monetary and fiscal policies.

The microeconomic logic for interest sensitivity of money demand was impeccable, essentially the same as the logic for the sensitivity of velocity to expected price inflation, a variable the monetarists deserve credit for reviving when Keynesians were neglecting it. The case is especially strong in a financial environment offering close interest-bearing substitutes for money. When this logic was accepted by Milton Friedman in his 1956 restatement of the quantity theory, it scarcely seemed controversial.[3] In 1959, however, Milton Friedman reported that he had not been able to detect empirically any significant interest rate effects on money demand.[4] He presented a theory, his permanent-income theory of the demand for money, designed to rationalize his empirical finding and to explain without the help of interest rates the observed procyclical fluctuations of velocity. As David Laidler[5] and Arthur Okun observed,[6] his was the only one of some twenty-two empirical studies on U.S. data that reached this conclusion. Friedman abandoned both his permanent-income theory of money demand and the interest-inelasticity proposition. In his essay on the *Optimum Quantity of Money*, interest sensitivity of money demand plays a central role.[7] And in 1966 he said, "... [No] 'fundamental issues' in either monetary theory or monetary policy hinge on whether the estimated elasticity [of demand for money with respect to interest rates] can ... be approximated by zero or is better approximated by -0.1 or -0.5 or -2.0, provided it is seldom capable of being approximated by $-\infty$."[8] This celebrated statement moved monetarist theory back to square one, confronting the inconsistency between endogenously flexible velocity and monetarist propositions about policy.

3. M. Friedman, "The Quantity Theory of Money: A Restatement," in *Studies in the Quantity Theory of Money*, Friedman, ed. (Chicago: University of Chicago Press, 1956); reprinted as Ch. 2, of his *Optimum Quantity of Money and Other Essays* (Chicago: Aldine, 1969).

4. M. Friedman, "The Demand for Money: Some Theoretical and Empirical Results," *Journal of Political Economy*, August 1959.

5. D. Laidler, "The Rate of Interest and the Demand for Money—Some Empirical Evidence," *Journal of Political Economy*, December 1966.

6. A. Okun, *The Political Economy of Prosperity* (Washington, D.C.: Brookings Institution, 1969), pp. 58, 146–47.

7. Friedman, *Optimum Quantity of Money*, Ch. 1.

8. Friedman, "Interest Rates and the Demand for Money," *Journal of Law and Economics*, October 1966; reprinted as Ch. 7 of his *Optimum Quantity of Money*.

2. *Infinite interest elasticity of real demand.* A different special case, still within the IS–LM framework, could provide a foundation for monetarist policy propositions. Even if the LM curve is not vertical, the IS curve could be horizontal. The real rate of interest would be fixed, not by the trap of absolute liquidity preference, but by perfect elasticity of aggregate demand for goods and services with respect to the interest rate. Given the expected inflation rate, real income is determined at the level that will equate the demand for real money balances at the fixed interest rate to the supply. Since fiscal measures cannot change the interest rate, they cannot alter the velocity of a given money supply. Additional government purchases, or additional private consumption induced by transfers or tax cuts, will completely "crowd out" pre-existing private demands for GNP. On the other hand, central bank actions increasing money supply will increase aggregate demand at existing prices, until output or prices or both rise enough to increase money demand correspondingly.

Perfect interest elasticity of aggregate demand could arise from several sources: capital investment, consumption, foreign investment (i.e., current account surplus). The domestic investment scenario is implausible. Even if the long-run schedule of marginal productivity of *capital* is very flat, as Frank Knight taught on the Midway, adjustment costs for individual firms and for the economy as a whole prevent massive short-run variations of *investment* in response to small deviations of short-term real interest rates. The consumption scenario likewise relies on an implausible degree of intertemporal substitution. The most plausible story is that of a small, open economy with a floating exchange rate and an interest rate determined abroad by the perfect substitutability of domestic and foreign assets. The standard Mundell–Fleming analysis of this case tells us that fiscal policy is impotent to alter aggregate demand, because its variations are wholly offset by the current external account.[9,10] However, this conclusion does not survive the inclusion of exchange-rate expectations, wealth effects, and imperfect asset substitution in the analysis.[11]

3. *Asset accumulation: dynamic effects.* Some critics of New Economics policy analysis questioned the Keynesian IS–LM framework, suggesting in particular that the indicated fiscal effects would be only temporary. With the passage of time, they argued, an expansionary fiscal policy unassisted by monetary expansion would continue to push interest rates up as savers' portfolios have to absorb a growing stock of nonmonetary government debt. Eventually this stock effect will nullify, or more than offset, the expansionary flow effect of the government spending or tax reduction. In graphical terms, the initial positive impact of an upward IS shift is overcome by subsequent upward and backward LM shifts.

The alleged Keynesian error was to ignore "the government budget restraint," i.e., the identity that over any finite time government deficits add to the stock of base money or to the stocks of nonmonetary public debt.[12] This argument appeared to provide a credible rationale

9. R. Mundell, "Capital Mobility and Stabilization Policy Under Fixed and Flexible Exchange Rates," *Canadian Journal of Economics and Political Economy*, November 1963, pp. 475–485; reprinted in his *International Economics*, Ch. 15.

10. M. Fleming, "Domestic Financial Policies Under Fixed and Floating Exchange Rates," *IMF Staff Papers*, November 1962, pp. 368–379.

11. J. Tobin and J. de Macedo, "The Short-Run Macroeconomics of Floating Exchange Rates: An Exposition," forthcoming in *Flexible Exchange Rates and the Balance of Payments: Essays in Memory of Egon Sohmen*, J. S. Chipman and C. P. Kindleberger, eds. (Amsterdam, North-Holland).

12. For example, see C. Christ, "A Simple Macroeconomic Model with a Government Budget Restraint," *Journal of Political Economy*, January/February 1968, pp. 53–67. Why he called the identity a restraint or even a constraint is a mystery.

for St. Louis Federal Reserve Bank "reduced-form" equations that showed the positive effects of fiscal stimuli petering out and turning negative after several quarters.[13]

On examination, however, the theoretical basis for the argument proved shaky. Suppose the reversal scenario occurs, so that after a temporary bulge the economy ends up with real income no higher than at the outset but with a higher interest rate. What induces the public to hold the money supply, by assumption unchanged? Not the income–interest combination—this reduces money demand. The answer must be that the public's wealth is greater. But will the public wish permanently to hold more wealth when its income is no higher and possibly lower? If not, its saving and consumption adjustments will take the economy to a higher income level. If so, the reason must be that demand for wealth is increased by the rise in the interest rate. But then why should the demand for money be greater? It is the interest rate on *non*monetary assets that has risen. There may be some portfolio-management reasons that demand for money rises with wealth, regardless of the motivation for the accumulation of wealth; but against these effects are the usual asset-substitution reasons for economizing cash balances when interest rates are high.[14]

Formal dynamic analysis of these stock-flow interactions did not substantiate the monetarist argument. Generally, an expansionary change of pure fiscal policy raises long-run equilibrium output, though by less than it raises output in the short run. However, dynamic models open a

13. L. C. Andersen and K. H. Carlson, "A Monetarist Model of Economic Stabilization," *Federal Reserve Bank of St. Louis Review*, April 1970.

14. J. Tobin, "Deficit Spending and Crowding Out in Shorter and Longer Runs," in *Theory for Economic Efficiency: Essays in Honor of Abba P. Lerner*, H. I. Greenfield et al., eds. (Cambridge, Mass.: M.I.T. Press, 1979), pp. 217-236.

wide range of possibilities, and monetarist scenarios cannot be excluded.[15]

4. *Government debt as deferred taxes: Ricardo–Barro as Modigliani–Miller.* Robert Barro has provided a theoretical argument against fiscal policy quite different from any of the preceding scenarios.[16] Reviving a Ricardian observation about deficit financing, Barro argues that the anticipation of future taxes to service public debt is as great a drag on current private spending as current payment of taxes. Taxpayers will not alter their consumption today or their planned consumption tomorrow when issue of interest-bearing debt replaces taxes in financing a given program of exhaustive government expenditure. In other words, the IS curve never shifts in the first place.

Monetary finance of government purchases is a wholly different phenomenon. Since monetary issue entails neither present nor future taxes, it increases the nominal wealth of private agents and leads them to demand more goods and services at prevailing prices. (Whether the new demand increases output or merely prices is another story.) By the same token, open-market operations substituting money for interest-bearing debt in portfolios increase nominal private wealth by erasing future tax obligations. This gives a rationale for Friedman's assertion that the origins of money supply, whether to purchase goods and services or to buy financial assets, are irrelevant. It does not give a rationale for treating inside money on a par with outside money.

15. A. S. Blinder and R. M. Solow, "Does Fiscal Policy Matter?", *Journal of Public Economics*, November 1973, pp. 319–337.
——, "Analytical Foundations of Fiscal Policy," in *The Economics of Public Finance* (Washington, D.C.: Brookings Institution, 1974), pp. 48–57.
J. Tobin and W. Buiter, "Long Run Effects of Fiscal and Monetary Policy on Aggregate Demand," in *Monetarism, Studies in Monetary Economics*, Vol. 1, J. L. Stein, ed. (Amsterdam: North-Holland, 1976).
16. R. Barro, "Are Government Bonds Net Wealth?", *Journal of Political Economy*, December 1974.

The Ricardo–Barro "equivalence theorem" refers to taxes and transfers, not to government purchases. The theory does not imply that purchases, whether financed by taxes or debt issue, will be offset by private behavior. A temporary increase in purchases, regarded by the public as a substitute neither for consumption nor for investment, would lead taxpayers to revise downward dollar for dollar their estimates of their wealth net of taxes. But they would spread the corresponding reduction of consumption over the long future, suffering only a small fraction concurrently with the government expenditure. In other words, the balanced-budget multiplier remains virtually intact.

The microeconomic assumptions underlying the Ricardo–Barro theorem are extreme and implausible. Essentially, consumer-taxpayers behave dynastically, as if they were immortal. Capital markets are perfect; the interest rate on government debt is available to private borrowers; nobody, now or in the future, is liquidity-constrained; taxes and transfers are lump-sum obligations or benefits; the government debt must not, and must not be perceived to, grow without bound. Deviations from these conditions restore the potential efficacy of fiscal policies. Moreover, an economy with Keynesian problems of underutilized resources is not a congenial environment for the Barro argument. The reason is that the employment of those resources can provide the incremental net wealth that would justify consumers in spending more when their current taxes are reduced. A Heller scenario would be a consistent self-fulfilling path.

Note that the Ricardo–Barro argument does not support the allegation that government debt issue crowds out investment, either domestic or foreign. The equivalence theorem says that debt issue crowds out consumption just as current taxation does. Since holding government securities is the perfect hedge against future taxes to service the debt, the Treasury can market its obligations without raising interest rates. Government purchases, of course, can crowd out other uses of resources.[17]

5. *Permanent income and consumption.* The Ricardo–Barro theorem is a special application of the permanent-income approach to consumption and saving behavior. The general approach is by no means fatal to fiscal policy, but it does suggest that multipliers for temporary compensatory fiscal measures are likely to be lower than old-fashioned consumption functions implied. In a pure, simple, extreme case an immortal or dynastic household consumes steadily the interest imputed to the present value of its net wealth, human and nonhuman. Previously anticipated changes in the after-tax incomes generated by those assets do not alter wealth calculations or consumption. Current income flows matter only as they convey new information about wealth. Temporary surprises alter wealth calculations very little, and consumption much less. Finite horizons, lifetimes or shorter, imply larger consumption responses to temporary income surprises. But anticipated income fluctuations should have no consequences for consumption.

Keynes himself had plenty to say about wealth and expectations in his discussion of consumption in Book III of the *General Theory.* But it is fair to say that textbook versions and early statistical implementations of multiplier theory were unduly mechanical and excessively liquidity-oriented, almost as if everyone were spending cash receipts hand-to-mouth or with a horizon of no longer than one year. The correction can be, and probably has been, over-

---

17. On these points, see J. Tobin, *Asset Accumulation and Economic Activity: Reflections on Contemporary Macroeconomic Theory*, Yrjo Jahnsson Lectures (Oxford: Basil Blackwell, 1980), Ch. 3.

done. Many households are liquidity-constrained. They do have short horizons, and their propensities to spend unexpected cash receipts, transient though they may be, are very high.

But what about *anticipated* receipts? After all, Heller and his colleagues were advocating compensatory fiscal policy. One of their proposals was to trigger increases in amount and duration of unemployment compensation by the overall unemployment rate. A favorite proposal, often repeated but never enacted, was a streamlined procedure for countercyclical variation of income tax rates by the President or Congress. Are compensatory measures doomed to failure once they are anticipated?

No doubt anticipation dilutes the stabilizing effects. The anticipation that government will provide income assistance in case of recessionary shock serves to augment consumption in prosperity as well as in recession. This is particularly true of individual entitlements, such as unemployment compensation. As in the case of retirement and medical insurance, individuals are spared part of the need for precautionary saving against the contingency. So far as the risk is insurable, the reduction in national saving is a welfare gain rather than a welfare loss. But some of the insured, e.g., young people without parental gifts or inheritances, will never have had the opportunity or liquidity to consume in advance the promised benefits. For them, the increase in consumption will occur during the recession, even though the benefits were anticipated. Moreover, when the government's commitment to compensatory countercyclical income generation is qualitative and global rather than quantitative and specific to individuals, then, assuming risk aversion, it is an imperfect substitute for individual precautions. For the actual beneficiaries, the government's income contributions will contain a large element of surprise. Once countercyclical income support, individual and global, has come to be expected, reversal of the policies would be a negative and destabilizing surprise.

6. *The new classical position: continuous macro-equilibrium.* My impression of monetarist theory, as it has evolved over the past fifteen years, is that it has embraced none of the above. Milton Friedman himself has not been content with any of the first five lines of argument, though elements of all of them occur in his writings. His main line of defense, in the last analysis, is the classical position that the economy is—or soon will be—in supply–demand equilibrium. Then, and only then, everything falls into place. Interest elasticities of money demand, investment, and saving do not matter. Fiscal measures just crowd out, not because the economy is money-constrained but because it is resource-constrained.

Friedman's natural rate doctrine asserted that no demand management policies, monetary or fiscal, could in the long run push the economy away from its Walrasian market equilibrium. His presidential address[18] left room for short-run disequilibria while repeating pragmatic doubts that policy interventions could speed or facilitate the adjustments. The new wave of monetarism, the new classical macroeconomics, equilibrium business cycle theory, have stated these propositions more categorically and provided for them a more persuasive intellectual foundation. I have argued elsewhere that the theory not only depends on implausible assumptions about the behavior of individual agents, the flexibility of prices in clearing markets, and the distribution of information, but also fails to explain well-established empirical regularities of business fluctuations.[19]

18. M. Friedman, "The Role of Monetary Policy," *American Economic Review*, March 1968; reprinted as Ch. 5 of *The Optimum Quantity of Money*.

19. References are given in the footnote[1] above on p. 12. Even better, see A. Okun, "Rational-Expectations-with-Misperceptions as a Theory of the Business Cycle," *Journal of Money, Credit, and Banking*, November 1980.

II. Stabilization Policy Then, 1961–65

The economy has not yet begun to recover from a sharp and quick recession, the third in a decade. The first came in the wake of a demoralizing war that divided the country and ended without victory. The second and the third were in large part the result of monetary and fiscal policies taken to keep inflation under control and to strengthen the dollar. The unemployment rate has been higher at each successive cyclical peak, and prevalent opinion Right and Left is that the economy is structurally doomed to high unemployment. The weakness of the dollar in foreign exchange is a source of weakness in the international monetary system and of anxiety all over the financial world, whose official and unofficial pundits warn the U.S. to put its house in order. They are particularly concerned about record peacetime federal budget deficits recently incurred. The American business community is suspicious of the federal government, even hostile. Businessmen feel over-regulated and overtaxed. Real investment is low, and the capital stock is old; the U.S. compares unfavorably on these scores with Germany, Japan, and other dynamic economies of the free world. Accelerated depreciation is the great cause that rallies businessmen. Consumers, workers, politicians, financiers share the pessimism of business about America's economic future. Postwar prosperity and growth seem to have burned out, condemning the country to uncontrollable cycles about an unsatisfactory trend.

This dismal account sounds like 1980–81, but it could have been written twenty years ago. Perhaps some of us have forgotten the crisis of confidence of the early 1960s; others are too young to remember or forget. Contrary to legend, the inauguration of John F. Kennedy did not usher in an era of good feeling among government, business, and labor and of confidence in America's economic future. It certainly did not bring consensus on macroeconomic policy. Walter Heller and his colleagues inspired deep suspicion and mistrust in influential business and financial circles, among trade union leaders, on Capitol Hill, and, not least, within the new administration itself.

The confrontation with the steel industry, the "Battle of Blough Run," didn't help the new president's standing with American business. The stock market plunged in 1962, losing 25 percent on the Standard and Poor industrial index prior to a long bull market beginning in the fall of the year. Business investors' sights were low, and corporate economists considered the council's estimates of the economy's potential and its prospects outrageously over-optimistic. Far from being an eagerly embraced new orthodoxy, the New Economics gained only gradual and grudging acceptance, as illustrated by the history of the Heller tax cut. Traditional doubts at Treasury, Federal Reserve, White House, Congress, and Wall Street delayed the proposal by the president and its enactment. Many of its eventual supporters emphasized not the demand management aspect of the tax reduction but its improvement of incentives for investment, risk-taking enterprise, and long-run growth. (Most economists today, I suspect, if they bothered to read or reread the official rationales of the Heller tax cut, would be surprised by the amount of "supply-side" language and argument.) The emphasis was, of course, not new; it had been the main economic motivation for the investment tax credit and the shortening of guidelines for depreciation in 1962.

In 1961, as today, fear of reigniting inflation was a major obstacle to the acceptance of stimulative demand management for recovery. Today this may seem hard to believe, given that the inflation rate was then around 1 percent per year. But re-acceleration to the 4–5-percent range of the mid-1950s was viewed as a political and economic disaster comparable to an acceleration from 9 to 15 percent or more today. It was to prevent this fear from immobilizing demand management and perpetuating stagnation that the administration, largely at the initiative of the Heller council, specifically of Kermit Gordon, intervened actively if informally in strategic wage negotiations and price decisions and promulgated the wage–price guideposts. Anyone who believes the legend that the council and the administration were deliberately and complacently riding up a naively misspecified Phillips curve should reexamine the history.

Walter Heller's signal achievement, as by consummate and patient persuasion he disarmed critics and skeptics internal and external and became the central architect of macro policy of the early 1960s, was to turn around the dismal economic prospect he, his president, and the nation faced at the beginning of the decade. The recovery of 1961–65 was not routine. Even if the continued prosperity of the Vietnam war period in the remainder of the decade is left out of account, Heller's recovery broke a dreary sequence of cyclical peaks with successively higher rates of unemployment, unhappily resumed in the 1970s. And through 1965 prosperity had not been purchased by significant increase in the inflation rate. The malaise, pessimism, and hostility that confronted the new administration in 1961 gave way to confidence and optimism. Fixed investment revived, and in 1965 was higher relative to GNP than in any postwar year. Coincidentally, the ratio of market value to replacement cost of corporate capital, sometimes known as "q", also set a postwar record, as yet unbroken, in 1965.

In demand management Heller had two objectives, one long run and one short run in nature. The long-run objective was to insure a realistic balance of national saving and

investment at full employment. The purpose was to make
the potential output of the economy attainable in actual
performance, to avoid chronic stagnation resulting from an
excess of potential national saving over investment. Heller's
diagnosis, "fiscal drag," called attention to the secular
growth of the full employment federal budget surplus.
Without the tax measures of the Kennedy–Johnson administration, net private domestic investment in 1965, 8 percent of GNP, would have had to exceed 10 percent of GNP
in order to absorb the national saving available. Moreover,
those tax measures must receive some of the credit for the
record rates of investment actually attained.

With hindsight it is easy to regret that federal revenues
were legislated away just prior to the burst of Vietnam War
spending. With cynicism bred in the 1970s, it is easy to
ridicule fears that presidents and Congresses of any political color will allow expenditures to lag behind revenues.
But fiscal drag was not a frivolous concern in the late
1950s and early 1960s. In fact, it is not a frivolous concern
today, when inflation combines with real growth to swell
potential federal receipts.

Heller and his council were well aware of the alternative
strategy, a mix of fiscal and monetary measures that would
use for investment the extra national saving afforded by
the growth of the high-employment federal surplus. Indeed, the investment tax credit and depreciation reform
were designed to tilt the composition of the gains in output during the recovery to investment rather than consumption. Civilian public investment, however attractive to
J. K. Galbraith and indeed to others of us personally, had
very limited appeal to the Congresses of the 1960s. To
increase the share of private investment in GNP another
two percentage points would have required an aggressively
easy monetary policy sustained for several years. In the
early stages of recovery, both excess capacity and pessi-

mism about final demand would be providing lots of slack in the string the monetary authorities would be pushing.

A more sophisticated bit of fine tuning would have stimulated demand by a temporary general tax cut, giving monetary ease the chance to take hold and leaving permanent room for high investment at full employment when the tax cut expired. I personally favored this approach, but that was before I understood the difficulty of explaning things to Congressman Wilbur Mills and Chairman William McChesney Martin.

Anyway, the decisive fact was that an aggressively easy monetary policy was not in the cards, no matter how tight the fiscal part of the policy mix. Even without a balance of payments constraint, it was probably never an option the Federal Reserve would buy. With the anxiety about the dollar and gold, the Fed and the Treasury felt it necessary to keep short-term rates at internationally competitive levels. As a result, they were higher in 1961 than in previous recession troughs. But, as described below, monetary policy accommodated the recovery, leaning less hard against the wind than in previous cycles. In this way, the Fed contributed to the strength of investment in the 1961–65 upswing.

The second objective of Heller macro policy was to diminish the amplitude of cyclical departures from the trend of full employment potential. Towards this end Heller prevailed on Presidents Kennedy and Johnson to ask Congress repeatedly either to delegate power to the president to initiate temporary changes in tax rates or to establish in advance procedures for rapid congressional action on specific proposals of previously agreed form. Although these recommendations got nowhere, they probably helped to create a climate in which antirecession tax reductions received fairly expeditious consideration. In view of the long delay in obtaining the 1968 surtaxes, the same cannot be said for anti-inflation tax increases. In addition to the tax proposals, and in the same spirit, the administration took various initiatives to make transfers, particularly unemployment compensation, more cyclically sensitive than they already were.

The Heller program emphasized the tax and transfer side of the budget rather than purchases. This emphasis reflected disillusionment with older notions that public works spending and other programs could be turned on and off on a timely schedule without great inefficiency. It also reflected the view of the "neoclassical synthesis" that governments' programs of exhaustive expenditures should be determined by judgment of permanent national priorities rather than by transient macroeconomic strategy.

Did these Heller proposals ignore the message of the permanent-income theory of consumption spending, discussed in Part I? I think not. The evidence was then, and I believe is still, that responses to temporary changes of disposable income are smaller than to permanent changes but still substantially positive.[20] The institution of regular countercyclical variation of tax rates is an extension of the "built-in stabilizers" of the fiscal system. As such, it helps to avoid temporary fluctuations of disposable income from cyclical shocks.

As I have argued elsewhere,[21] a more powerful tax stabilizer would provide direct incentive to substitute outlays in periods of low activity and employment for outlays in prosperities. Systematic cyclical variation of excises on consumer durables is one device. Another is cyclical varia-

---

20. F. Modigliani and C. Steindel, "Is a Tax Rebate an Effective Tool for Stabilization Policy?" and "Discussion," *Brookings Papers on Economic Activity*, vol. 1, 1977, pp. 175–210. The article reviews the issues and the empirical findings and presents estimates from macroeconometric models and the authors' own equations.

21. Tobin, *The New Economics One Decade Older*, pp. 80–82.

tion of the investment tax credit. In both cases, the effectiveness of the device in inducing stabilizing intertemporal substitution is enhanced by its anticipation.

Why not leave short-term countercyclical stabilization to monetary policy? There were and are several reasons. First, although the inside lag is shorter than for fiscal measures, the lag between stimulative action and macroeconomic result is long and, yes, variable; the payoff from "pushing on a string" is uncertain and slow. On the other hand, monetary restriction pushed hard enough to produce a credit crunch that reverses the economy's direction acts quickly but severely. Second, the monetary authorities have to temper their dedication to domestic stabilization by concern for the balance of payments and the foreign exchanges. Third, the political and quasi-constitutional fact is that anyone sitting in the White House and Executive Office feels that monetary weapons are not in his arsenal. Confronting this fact, he naturally stresses fiscal management and fiscal architecture.

The monetary stance of 1961–65 was described then and is describable now as a "bill rate only" policy, the label differentiating it from the ruling "bills only" doctrine of the Eisenhower years. In the early 1960s the Fed set target bill rates, largely dictated by judgments of what was required to avoid outflows of short-term financial capital. Reserves were supplied in the quantities demanded at these rates. The target bill rate was gradually raised during the recovery. But as Figures 1 and 2 illustrate, interest rates rose less and real monetary quantities grew more than in most previous and subsequent recovery periods. The Fed leaned less strongly against the wind.

A secondary dimension of monetary policy in the Heller recovery was the Fed's grudging abandonment of "bills only." On occasion the Fed purchased longer-term securities in the open market. The purpose was to "twist" the

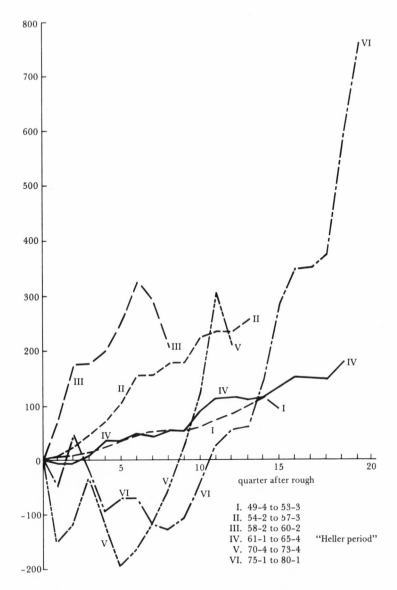

Figure 1 Treasury bill rate in six recoveries, difference (in basis points) from rate at start of recovery.

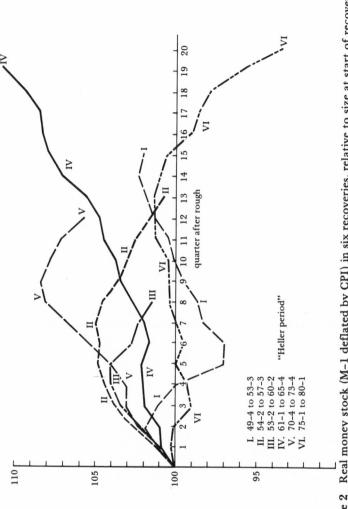

Figure 2 Real money stock (M-1 deflated by CPI) in six recoveries, relative to size at start of recovery.

term structure in a direction more favorable to domestic investment but, it was hoped, less vulnerable to international capital outflow. Whatever small effect these efforts might have had, they were more than offset by Treasury refunding operations in the reverse direction, designed to increase the average maturity of federal debt. "Twist" was more effectively obtained by two other devices: increasing ceiling rates on deposits, drawing into intermediaries funds that were re-lent in the mortgage market, and imposing Robert Roosa's "interest equalization tax," a tariff on foreign placements of securities in the U.S. market.

The accommodative stance of the Federal Reserve in this period, strongly encouraged by the administration, shows that Heller and his colleagues were not pure "fiscalists" by any means. For Keynesians, however, the passivity of the Fed was indicative that the driving forces of recovery arose from nonmonetary sources, including both fiscal policy and the revival of confidence among business investors and consumers. A classic identification problem remains. For example, Art Okun spelled out the evidence that the Heller tax cut shifted the IS curve to the right.[22] But would it have raised income and employment if the Fed had been unwilling to let the LM curve drift righward too? And if, without the tax cut and other fiscal measures, the Fed had increased reserves, or M-1, or some other monetary indicator by the same amount, would the growth of income and employment have been any less? To these questions, which Friedman[23] and other monetarists asked, the Heller experiment does not provide an answer. The answer depends on the shape of the LM locus, an issue

22. A. Okun, "Measuring the Impact of the 1964 Tax Reduction," in *Perspectives on Economic Growth*, W. Heller, ed. (New York: Random House, 1968).

23. M. Friedman and W. Heller, *Monetary vs. Fiscal Policy: A Dialogue* (New York: Norton, 1969), pp. 55-56.

discussed elsewhere in the paper. Certainly, with what we know about money supply and demand during the period, the recorded statistical association between money and income cannot be regarded as a causal link that policymakers could exploit, any more than the recorded association between fiscal stimuli and income could be expected to be repeated in a different monetary environment.

In 1980 retrospect, more than at the time, the most remarkable feature of the 1961-65 recovery was the modest degree of wage and price acceleration. My suspicion is that guideposts and open-month policies deserve more credit than cynical observers have been disposed to give them. Of course they could not and did not succeed or survive in the subsequent period of excess demand.

In Table I, I have compared the Heller recovery (IV, truncated at the fourth quarter of 1965) with the five other postwar cyclical recoveries in the United States. Considering its length, the degree of real output growth, the reduction of unemployment, and the low level of unemployment attained, the small amount of price accleration and the deceleration of total hourly compensation are remarkable. Recall that recovery I covers the Korean War period, during which deceleration of wages and prices was accomplished with the help of controls, while the wage and price record of the most recent recovery, VI, is colored by the OPEC bulges that preceded it and accompanied its final days.

III. Stabilization Policy Now, 1981-?

During the first half of the 1960s the mean performance of the economy improved and its variance declined. These were the objectives of the Heller revolution in macroeconomic policy. The fates were kind, to be sure, but the

Table I Six Postwar U.S. Recoveries: Summary Statistics

Recovery:	I	II	III	IV	V	VI
Dates, by quarters trough to peak	49–4 to 53–3	54–2 to 57–3	58–2 to 60–2	61–1 to 65–4*	70–4 to 73–4	75–1 to 80–1
Duration, quarters	15	13	8	19	12	20
Real GNP in final quarter relative to trough	1.27	1.13	1.11	1.29	1.16	1.24
GNP price deflator, annual percentage rate of increase:						
8 quarters prior to trough	0.97	1.81	2.61	1.33	5.43	10.04
First 4 quarters of recovery	5.34	1.84	2.43	2.03	4.41	4.92
Last 4 quarters of recovery	1.90	3.48	1.78	2.46	7.50	8.93
Unemployment rate:						
Trough quarter	7.0	5.8	7.4	6.8	5.9	8.6
Final quarter	2.7	4.2	5.2	4.1	4.8	6.1
Difference	4.3	1.6	2.2	2.7	1.1	2.5
Total Compensation per hour, percentage annual rate of increase:						
8 quarters prior to trough	4.29	5.05	5.02	3.92	6.44	9.57
First 4 quarters of recovery	8.77	3.78	4.59	4.37	5.87	9.17
Last 4 quarters of recovery	6.07	5.64	4.39	3.65	10.17	9.02

*The period for the "Heller recovery" is terminated prior to the Vietnam War escalation, thus prior to the cyclical peak.

Note: Identification of series, with series number from *Business Conditions Digest*. Gross National Product in 1972 dollars, no. 50. Unemployment rate, total, no. 43. Implicit price deflator, Gross National Product, no. 310. Index of average hourly compensation, all employees, nonfarm business sector, no. 345.

results were not just accidental. The policies worked. Equally important, a consensus of understanding of the aims and roles of government and private sectors was achieved, and confidence in the nation's economic future was restored. Now when our need is even more acute, could the Heller magic work again?

In the climate of pessimism that pervades the country and our profession, it is easy to list ways in which the environment of stabilization policy will be worse in January 1981 than in January 1961: energy and OPEC, the plight of the dollar in foreign exchange markets, the competitive weakness of major American industries, the vanishing of productivity growth, the lag in capital accumulation and the narrowing of margins of usable idle capital capacity accompanying increases in unemployment of labor, the destruction of the earlier consensus about stabilization policies. I have recently reviewed at some length the impact of economic and professional developments of the 1970s on demand management, and I shall not repeat the story here.[24] But I am certainly not convinced that these events doom the economy of the 1980s to stop-go cycles around a stagflationary trend.

Oil price hikes were shocks in the 1970s. But now increases in the dollar price and relative price of oil can no longer be surprises, even if they occur in discrete jumps. Suppose the trend of the relative price of oil is the real rate of interest available to OPEC, say 5 percent per year. If our oil imports are 5 percent of GNP, the net result is equivalent to a ¼ of 1 percent per year decline of productivity, and to a similar increase in the margin between price inflation and growth of domestic nominal incomes. This should not be beyond the capacity of policymakers and

24. J. Tobin, "Stabilization Policy Ten Years After," *Brookings Papers on Economic Activity*, vol. 1, 1980, pp. 19-72.

private agents to anticipate. Meanwhile, we are in our muddled democratic way making real progress toward energy conservation. Now and in the future we have less costly and more discriminating ways than wholesale recessions to hold our demands within OPEC supply limits. Likewise, by now the technology for energy-saving and energy-producing investments has had time to develop, and such investments can go a long way toward remedying the weakness of capital formation.

Although the floating dollar, and the possibility of recurrent speculative attacks upon it, will continue to be a concern of U.S. policymakers, there are silver linings to this cloud too. American exports are benefiting from the portfolio preferences that have valued other currencies above purchasing power parities. Although floating rates have not liberated national macro policies from international constraints, as some economists may erroneously have promised, they permit at least as much freedom of action as the Bretton Woods system did and they have relieved this country of the panicky anxieties about gold of the 1960s. Somebody makes monetary policy for the world as a whole, even when central banks are acting at cross purposes. The U.S. certainly has a large weight. *Our* central bank need not feel that it has no control over world and domestic interest rates.

Structural shifts in the composition of output—responding to relative prices, international comparative advantage, and other trends—are nothing new. They do not make macroeconomic stabilization impossible. Conversely, recession and stagnation impede the necessary readjustments. We cannot run the economy at such high pressure that sinking industries remain afloat, but neither does the whole economy have to sink because Detroit has mismanaged its competitive race with Japanese automobile makers.

Slogans are cheap, but no one has a recipe for accelerating productivity. We don't even know the sources of its recent slowdown, or to what extent they are the transient consequences of the extraordinary economic history of the 1970s. My guess is that stable expansion in the 1980s would revive jointly capital investment and productivity. Timid stagnation, on the other hand, may well be a self-defeating strategy, a self-fulfilling prophecy of decline. Holding economic activity and employment down in order to preserve margins of excess capacity deprives business firms of the main incentive to expand and deteriorates the country's stock of human capital.

The Heller strategy of the 1960s was not a one-sided program of demand expansion. It held forth the prospect of expanding markets combined with tax incentives and a benign financial climate for investment, and with manpower and labor market measures to diminish structural and frictional unemployment. Although there is merit in some of the "supply-side" proposals so popular today, the danger is that they are considered a substitute for expanding demand. As in the early 1960s, it is hard to suppress the suspicion that business and financial interests seek to gain from tax concessions the profits that in a growing economy they would earn from expansion. Likewise, some business leaders seem reconciled to chronically tight monetary conditions so long as they can escape the bite by tax relief.

In the end, I think, the really big difference between 1981 and 1961 is nine points of core inflation. Give the two Eisenhower–Martin recessions of 1957–8 and 1960 credit for the favorable initial condition that greeted Heller and Kennedy on inauguration day. The recessions of the 1970s have not done the same job for their counterparts next January. The principal barriers to a Heller-like program of coordinated demand and supply expansion in the

1980s are the general fear of accelerating the inflation and the obligatory political commitment to reducing it. A pessimistic prognosis for the decade would be the continuation of stop–go cycles, with ever higher peak and average unemployment rates and with little or no net growth of real output. In this scenario policy-induced recessions, triggered by inflationary bulges as in 1975 and 1979, never achieve permanent disinflation. But the fear of reigniting inflation inhibits antirecession and recovery policies. Faced with this alternative, some economists might vote for a Heller scenario in the 1980s even if it meant continuation of 8-10-percent inflation for sure plus risks of further acceleration. Realistically, given the national and international politics of macroeconomic policies, this option is not in the cards.

The alternative, as I have argued on several other occasions,[25] is to engineer an organized disinflation of wages and prices, consistent with a disinflation of nominal aggregate demand. This could be done by an agreed and announced schedule of annually declining guideposts, with tax-based inducements for firms, workers, and unions to comply. Incomes policy was a central part of the Heller strategy of 1961-65, and it is even more crucial today. The task is more formidable, not just holding the line but lowering it. That is why the open mouth needs teeth. It is also why the policy requires a consensus within government, among Federal Reserve, administration, and Congress, and a social consensus among government, management, and labor. But the main requirement is firm, imaginative, foresighted, and bold presidential leadership, for which the early months of 1981 provide a rare opportunity.

25. J. Tobin, "Stabilization Policy Ten Years After," *Brookings Papers on Economic Activity*, vol. 1, 1980, pp. 66-71.

Paul A. Samuelson:
Comment (Post-Camelot Dilemmas)

James Tobin's talk is a hard act to comment on. He makes no interesting mistakes. His calm judiciousness is truly offensive. All I can do is retaliate in kind, repaying his wisdom with further wisdom.

Let me begin with crude monetarism. When Bob and Bobbie Solow were having their house built on Martha's Vineyard, Bob asked the contractor if he was a native islander. "That's the only kind there is," was the reply. I speak of crude monetarism because that's the only kind there is. When a person who wears the badge of monetarist goes beyond a black-box model in which it is asserted that the output nominal GNP or the price level does, damn it, depend on the input of aggregate money supply; when the mechanism inside the black box is analyzed and explained; when the reasonable neoclassical properties of prudent cash-balance management are investigated; in short, when the totality of the macro evidence is given careful analytical interpretation by a monetarist, the monetarist turns out to be a post-Keynesian. I am speaking of Milton Friedman, and of Brunner and Meltzer. Their written-down systems, when put through a Jacobian tester, turn out to be isomorphic with a Modigliani Mark VI model.

Am I speaking of Robert Lucas, Neil Wallace, Tom Sargent, and Robert Barro? These rational expectationists—particularly when they are on their guard and do not deviate into good sense—are proudly crude monetarists. Their essential contention is that any increase in the stock of M does *very soon* result in a proportionate increase in all prices, being neutral except in the shortest run with respect to real variables of production, employment, and relative prices, real incomes and real interest rates. Thus far the *empirical* evidence for the comparative static of the rational expectationists has been weak—indeed weaker than I suspect will eventually be found to be the true merits of their *Weltanschauung*.

All of the above is by way of making the following point: It is not the case that monetarism has been found scientifically to be a better paradigm than 1965 Keynesianism. The case is not convincing that the velocity of money is a hard exogenous constant or parameter. Money creation via gold discoveries or via showering down from helicopters is not putatively of the same quantitative potency as money creation from open-market operations that substitute interest-bearing debt for currency. Taxes and deficit financing of expenditures do not reasonably have the same effects upon current demand spending.

Why then does the world not expect that the methods that Walter Heller and the Camelot crew used would be as useful today as they were then? Indeed, why is it that we who answer to the same drum beat as Walter Heller would not expect the problems of the 1980s to yield to the methods that worked so well then? I don't think the answers can be found in the shapes of the IS and LM diagrams, and in the differences of opinions about their shapes that are sometimes associated with the debaters who call themselves monetarists and those who don't. What goes on outside the diagrams relating nominal money, nominal income levels, and nominal interest rates is an important part of the modern dilemma. We modern sophisticated Keynesians are as critical of various verions of old-fashioned Keynesianism as monetarists are. But that does not make us monetarists. Someone who had heard that George Santayana was a lapsed Catholic asked him if it was true he had turned Protestant. Santayana replied, "Sir, I have lost my faith, not my reason."

The period 1961–65 was too lucky a period to be extrapolatable. Three recessions during Eisenhower's two terms, plus a trend of real growth that averaged only about 2-½ percent per year, meant that President Kennedy inherited an economy that was exceptionally free of the disease of stagflation. We had visible and invisible reservoirs of labor, visible and invisible slack in capital stock. The opposition of Congress to activistic macro policies of expansion, coupled with the initial doubts of the new President himself and the active internal opposition to activism from within the administration, combined to make the expansion a slow one. Sometimes it seems that slow expansions make for steady expansions of long duration.

Perhaps Jim Tobin remembers an argument between us just before Inauguration Day, 1961. I was more pessimistic than he was concerning how much the economy could expand before running into induced price inflation. I was under the influence of Alvin Hansen, Lord Beveridge, and other Keynesians who from 1945 on doubted that a modern mixed economy could simultaneously enjoy the following three benefits: full employment, stable price level, and "free" wage bargaining uncontrolled by peacetime governmental price and wage controls. We each made a pencil sketch of our predicted pattern of induced price-level change—so to speak of our respective short-term Phillips curves—and my horoscope was the gloomier of the two.

Not for the first or last time, Samuelson turned out to be wrong and Tobin turned out to be right. Kennedy cum Heller did get the country moving again and yet with comparatively little heating up of the economy. Only after 1965, in the age of Johnson rather than Kennedy, did my apprehensions turn out to be only too well founded. It is worth thinking about why the 1961–65 period was a luckier one than we would have a right to expect in the steady state.

I've mentioned the state of the system inherited from Eisenhower. That's one basic factor. Also, I have to agree with Tobin that the wage–price guideposts, concerning which I had been skeptical when Walt Rostow had propagandized for them in pre-Election times, did perform an independent useful role. Once business and labor did act with moderation, that made it easier for them and the system to enjoy expansions in real magnitudes of an unusual amount relative to the concomitant expansions in price and wage tags. The fact that America was politically stuck with an overvalued dollar, and that the rest of the world preferred to take in our dollar IOUs to appreciating their currencies, undoubtedly helped moderate our rate of inflation. Tax reductions, promised and realized, may also have helped to keep costs down.

As one reviews these favorable factors, one realizes that we were not in an equilibrium system that could have been permanently or for a long time maintained. Even in the absence of the disastrous Vietnam War and President Johnson's rejection of his economists' advice on how to finance it, as the 1960s developed I believe we would have run into the problem of overheating and incipient stagflation—although not in the malevolent form of the Vietnam epoch. History is a one-time thing and I cannot prove my point. But my contention is consistent with what we have been observing abroad these last 15 years and with our own experiences in the 1970s.

The problem of stagflation is of course what I have in mind. It is a problem that negates simple Keynesianism more cogently than the hypotheses and claims of any of the schools of monetarism. It colors almost all of our macroeconomic policy decisions.

Here are two quite different examples. Tobin has mentioned the wish of Kennedy–Johnson economists that Congress would act to make possible countercyclical tax rates that come into effect automatically. That is a commendable if utopian goal. However, as one reviews the recessions since the early 1970s, one realizes that it is not the case that they last too long because government is unable to get the proper tax reductions into effect except after a wasteful lag. On the contrary. The last two recessions have been recessions deliberately contrived by government. An autumn 1980 poll of economists would show that as many of them are worried that the recession *will not last long enough* as are worried that it will last too long.

Since January 1979 economists have known that production is stagnating and unemployment threatening to rise. Were it not for the desire by much of the American establishment to fight inflation and its possible acceleration by means of keeping economic growth deliberately weak, there would have been plenty of time to legislate discretionary tax cuts. The lags intrinsic to the legislative process, and the shortening of such lags by the setting up of automaticity in tax rates, have played no critical role in the business cycle associated with the stagflation of recent times.

My second example to show how stagflation altered the importance of various issues has to do with the ability or inability of economic science to forecast the future. Even if the evidence had convinced Friedman that fiscal policy could have effects on aggregate demand comparable to those of monetary policy, he would have argued against discretionary macroeconomic policy. His case for mandatory rules rather than intelligent discretionary stabilization programs ultimately rests on his hatred of a system of men as against a system of impersonal law. Friedman would be

the unhappiest person if his researches led to the finding
that feasible stabilization policies can be found that will
work well. But there is no danger that such a finding will
bludgeon its way into his consciousness. When his calculations turn up an R^2 of $1/2$, his eye perceives this as a
$1-R^2$ of $1/2$. Because of the long and variable lags involved, because of the noise in the data, because of the forecasting fallibility of economists, any attempt to depart
from a rule of constant growth in the money supply (and
from an equivalent rule in fiscal policy for those who believe in fiscal policy) will, it is argued, actually do more
harm than good. When one studies by means of optimal-
control theory how special are the properties of a system
and of its exogenous noise that will lead to the optimality
of a rule of constancy of the money supply, those who
have not Friedman's philosophical axe to grind may be
skeptical of the cogency of his critique and of its last line
of defense in the form of the allegation, "even if a jury of
economists could improve on the rule of steady growth,
the perversity of democracy and Congress will guarantee
that they will not be listened to."

All the above has been important in the history of
macroeconomic policy debates. My present point is that
most of it is quite irrelevant to the dilemmas thrown up by
current-day stagflation. It is not the case that we fail to
take expansive action because we mistakenly think the system is stronger than it really is. It is not the case that we
fail to take contractionary action because we mistakenly
think the system is weaker than it really is. The present
human condition in the United States and the other mixed
economies is that almost all of the time we are subjected
to schizoid temptations: we are stopped from engineering
the macroeconomic stimuli that will undoubtedly help the
unemployment and production situation by the fear that
this will make impossible the tempting macroeconomic

restrictions that will undoubtedly put some downward pressure on the rate of inflation. If Providence laid out before us exactly what the future would be like under each pattern of policy programming, stagflation would still leave us debating what ought to be done.

I hate to talk in this vein. How nice it would be to banish defeatism, to talk in upbeat tones. But scientific truth does have its solemn obligations.

At the same time humane goals remain an abiding concern. While not kidding ourselves concerning the efficacy and feasibility of various incomes-policies innovations, the stakes are so high and the losses from stagnation are so serious that I must applaud scientific researches into new and improved modes of incomes policy.

Thus, for some 18 months prior to January 1980, Norway had price and wage controls. To my surprise, it seems to have worked pretty well. Now, eight months later, Norwegian unemployment is at an unbelievable level of 15,000 workers. The Norwegian wage and price level is indeed beginning to heat up, but not in a way that needs to be explained by an *aftermath* of the control period rather than by current overfull employment alone.

Norway is not America. But open-minded monitoring rather than close-minded ideology is still in order—in the good Heller manner.

Where have all the Flowers Gone? Economic Growth in the 1960s

Robert M. Solow

The first serious attempt to give concrete content to the concept of potential output was one of Arthur Okun's important and enduring legacies to macroeconomic analysis. The establishment of potential output as the appropriate standard and target for stabilization policy in a fluctuating economy is one of Walter Heller's important and, I hope, enduring contributions to the theory and practice of macroeconomic policy.

The generation of macroeconomists that came of age after the Heller years cannot possibly imagine how useful and refreshing it was, only twenty years ago, to have a workable alternative to the ups-and-downs approach to economic stabilization, according to which things are good whenever they are getting better and bad whenever they are getting worse. The familiar corollary is that no one can legitimately complain when GNP and employment are "setting new records." Perhaps I exaggerate, but only trivially. Okun's work, trying to measure potential GNP and account for the variation of actual GNP around it, and Heller's work, interpreting the injunction of the Employment Act in a meaningful and practical way, were a breath of fresh air.

The concept of potential output has another role to play in practical macroeconomic analysis. It is the key variable in descriptions and theories of economic growth. We would want to be able to measure and talk about potential output even if short-term stabilization were of no concern. It would still be important, for example, to be able to estimate the effect of changes in investment on the path of potential output, even in the absence of business cycles.

It is therefore no surprise that practically-minded macroeconomists in the U.S. continued to analyze and track potential GNP during the 1960s and 1970s. For instance, Perry[1] and Nordhaus[2] carried on the Okun tradition, refining the concept by disaggregation and otherwise, extending the range of data and statistical methods, and looking forward as well as backward.

Okun's original work had estimated the growth rate of potential GNP to be 3-½ percent a year from the mid-1950s to the early 1960s, and that was the canonical number at the Heller council. Perry and Nordhaus shared the common view that potential growth had accelerated in the late 1960s, perhaps to 4-¼ percent annually, with faster labor-force growth more than offsetting a small productivity slowdown. Looking ahead to the 1970s, Perry rather expected the faster growth to be maintained. His work, which emphasized the demographic disaggregation of employment, tended to attribute any slight deterioration in the rate of productivity advance to an adverse shift in the age–sex composition of the labor force. If and when that shift leveled off—indeed, the age shift could be expected to do more, and actually to reverse itself—the productivity trend should be expected to resume its earlier rate of increase. Nordhaus, on the other hand, projected that growth of potential would fall back to 3-½ percent a year in the 1970s. His work, which emphasized

1. G. Perry, *Brookings Papers on Economic Activity*, 1971.
2. W. Nardhaus, *Brookings Papers on Economic Activity*, 1972.

the industrial disaggregation of employment and output, attributed any slight deterioration in the rate of productivity advance to an adverse shift in the composition of output toward low-productivity industries. Since that shift, a matter of income and price elasticities of demand, was expected to continue, there would be no rebound in the productivity trend.

The reconciliation of these apparently contrasting views comes from the coincidence that Nordhaus's low-productivity industries are the ones that absorb a large fraction of Perry's women and youths. In effect, Nordhaus's conclusion rested on the assumption that workers of any demographic aspect will have low productivity in low-productivity industries. Perry's conclusion rested on the assumption that high-productivity demographic groups will carry their high productivity into whatever industry employs them. In the event, as we know, the productivity trend deteriorated further; but industry-compositional effects do not seem to have been the major factor.

Ten years later, we think that one of the most important economic events of the 1970s was a drastic slowdown in the productivity component of potential growth. The 1979 *Economic Report* put the growth of potential at 3 percent a year from 1973-78 and projected the same rate of growth for the five years 1978-83. One year later the *Report* lowered its projection for 1979-81 to 2-½ percent, but held to the 3 percent figure for 1982-85, with about 1-¾ percent a year expected to come from a somewhat improved productivity performance and the remaining 1-¼ percent from the growth of hours worked. Other projections are in the same ballpark. DRI is a bit more pessimistic, but such small differences are mostly guesswork.

There is now a substantial literature on the productivity puzzle: what happened, when it happened, and why it happened. Nordhaus's 1972 paper was already entitled

"The Recent Productivity Slowdown," Perry returned to the subject in 1977;[3] Norsworthy, Harper, and Kunze studied it most recently in 1979 (with many references);[4] and, of course, that sort of thing is Denison's native habitat. It is debated whether the productivity slowdown, or at least the part of it that is not explicable by other identifiable developments, began in 1965 or 1969 or 1973 and whether it came in one or two stages. (The intrinsically more plausible hypothesis of a gradual deceleration gets generally low grades, either because it is not true or because it would be asking too much of short time series regressions to pick it up even if it is there.) The other main enterprise in the literature is the decomposition of the overall productivity trend into additive components attributable to cyclical factors, to changes in the "quality" of the labor force, to movements in the stock of plant and equipment, to changes in the terms on which the economy has access to energy, and to still other factors.

I do not intend to add to that literature. To be honest, I suspect that continued reworking of the same old data, supplemented by the few new observations provided by the calendar—which continues to go by at approximately one year per year—is not a good thing. I am less and less able to convince myself that this iterative process converges, or even that it gets closer to the truth as it goes along. I would like to think that this skepticism reflects a reasoned feeling that there is an intrinsic limit to the refinement of the answers that you can get by asking delicate questions of short aggregative time series, whereas much longer time series cannot be presumed to be appropriately stationary. But perhaps it is just grumpiness.

3. Perry, *Brookings Papers on Economic Activity*, 1977.

4. Norsworthy, Harper, and Kunze, *Brookings Papers on Economic Activity*, 1979.

In any case, my plan is to look back at the 1960s and, to a lesser extent, the 1970s, from the point of view of the Heller council, with its hopes, its fears, and its intellectual preconceptions. The object is not to assign grades; it goes without saying that we did not foresee the surprises of the 1970s. But it may be instructive to review those events against the backdrop of a reasonably consistent, if now slightly dated, approach to short-run and long-run macroeconomics. There may even be some fresh insights to be had.

The Heller council took economic growth seriously, as a subject for analysis and as an object for policy. As a prelude to looking at the events of the 1960s and 1970s, through the council's eyes, I want to reconstruct some of the ideas that guided our approach to the subject. It brings me up short to realize that, in 1961, only yesterday, the models of economic growth proposed by Tobin and me were only five years old. They were part of our mental furniture; and the upholstery was hardly worn.

We drew a sharp distinction between *growth*, which meant the increase in potential output, and *gap-closing*, which meant changes in real output relative to potential. That is obvious to us now, but in those days common parlance tended to describe all increases in real GNP as "growth." I regret to say that common parlance has not become much more accurate over the years. The distinction is not merely parochial; discussion of macroeconomic policy can only be confused by a failure to distinguish between fluctuations in the GNP gap, which are primarily a reflection of fluctuations in aggregate demand, and movements of the potential trend, which are a matter of the supply of aggregate output. ("Supply-side economics" is hardly new, only its current punk-rock version.) As readers of Harrod and Domar, we were of course aware that events

like plant and equipment spending had both demand-side
and supply-side consequences.

In 1961 and 1962, the council tended to give priority to
gap-closing. We were then—I speak for myself—unaware
that, since the unemployment rate was running at 6.8 percent in the first half of 1961, the natural rate of unemployment must be 6.8 percent. To us, unemployment
seemed undesirably, even "unnaturally," high. With GNP
falling 8 percent short of potential, narrowing the gap
seemed more immediately urgent than adding a half a
point to the trend growth of potential. Besides, there was
general agreement that a tighter economy was a necessary
precondition of rapid growth.

But then why promote accelerated growth at all? In the
1962 *Economic Report* the council gave two reasons. The
first, in a nutshell, was that faster growth would provide
"room" for the reduction of poverty without the divisive-
ness that would probably be aroused by an attempt to redistribute a more nearly stagnant aggregate income. A
rapidly-growing, and fully employed, economy would absorb some of the disadvantaged into jobs, and would find
it easier to provide a decent level of transfer payments for
the old, the infirm, and the incapable as well as education
and training for their children. We included also a wish list
of worthy causes and public and mixed public-private
goods and services, to which the political process would
presumably be more willing to devote a constant fraction
of a growing total than a rising fraction of a fixed sum.
The emphasis was clearly guided by the belief that a society would more likely do good if it were doing well.

The second justification for rapid growth was international. There were some sentences about the "military
security of the free world"; growth would also provide
"room" for military expenditure. Of course things were
different then. We did not know that whatever room there

was, and more, would be used up five years later in Vietnam. I note that those sentiments are back in fashion again, and I leave their evaluation to others. The *Report* also said something about the ability of a growing U.S. economy to provide resources, an example, and markets for the poor countries of the world. Those sentiments have never been in fashion, and at this distance there is a perfunctory air about the passage.

Of course economists distinguish between the conviction that economic growth is a good thing and the conclusion that it is a legitimate object of public policy. The Heller council and its staff thought about that. There was discussion about likely divergences between the private and social risk attached to plant and equipment decisions, about the inadequacy of private markets in the financing of investment in human capital, and about the public-good element in research and development. Tobin's Ely lecture on "Economic Growth as an Object of Government Policy" exemplifies the intellectual framework. But the 1962 *Report* was already carrying a heavy educational load and we spared the waiting world a lesson in intertemporal welfare economics. I think there was also a background feeling that a country might make a "corporate" decision in favor of faster growth, in much the same way that people who would not volunteer for military service might vote for conscription to which they would, as individuals, be subject.

Chapter 2 of the 1962 *Report* covered most of the waterfront. There were sections on human resources, technological progress, natural resources, public services, and housing. In each instance we discussed past trends, significance for growth, and possible policies. But our heart was in plant and equipment investment. We felt on sounder ground, analytically; we thought the payoff would be quicker and surer; and we had some policy ideas.

Council thinking took account of the standard growth-theory pessimism about investment. A higher ratio of investment to GNP brings only a temporary bulge in the growth rate, which eventually decays back to the "natural rate." And the elasticity of output with respect to the stock of physical capital is pretty small. But we drew some optimism from the idea that "embodiment" effects might be important; and we had the rough insight, which only later got into formal modeling, that higher investment in a "putty-clay" world would induce the transfer of labor from older low-productivity to newer high-productivity capital. So we concluded that the response of potential output to higher investment would be tolerably large and quick. The investment tax credit and revision of the guidelines for the tax lives of depreciable assets quickly became part of the administration's program. It is a little ironic that those items were accomplished before the big tax reduction of 1964, despite the council's explicit arguments that nothing would do much good until there was a major increase in aggregate demand, spontaneous or engineered. (In fact, nothing did.) The *Report* also argued the standard case that, for any given level of aggregate demand, a mix of tight fiscal and easy monetary policy would favor investment spending over public and private consumption. Apparently, no one was listening, to judge from the subsequent history.

There is one undocumented episode worth recalling. We had the notion of trying informally the weakest sort of "indicative planning," in the hope that the pooling of information might reduce the risks associated with capital expansion. We drew up a sort of questionnaire that might conceivably have been distributed to large companies, trade associations, and financial institutions. The general intent was to describe alternative scenarios in terms of GNP aggregates, perhaps with some tentative breakdown of demand by broad sector, and then ask each respondent to fill in its own industry-demand estimates and probable capital-expenditure response to each hypothetical market situation. Our idea was that the responses would give us some information as to which of the scenarios were internally consistent, in the sense that they would evoke the expenditures that would actually bring them about. Moreover, the responses could be aggregated (enough to provide privacy) and reported back iteratively to the respondents, who might then reply, "Oh, in that case I would actually do something a bit different from what I reported on the first round without this information." It seems a harmless, not to say naive, exercise. But this piece of incipient *dirigisme* was felt to be impossibly subversive by those we talked to inside the administration and in the private sector. We dropped the whole scheme.

The 1962 *Report* set "goals" for the 1960s. A goal is some sort of convex combination of a hope, an intention, and an expectation; goal-setting was a popular indoor sport in those days. The council was trying to estimate what was possible with fairly strong policies aimed especially at the accumulation of human and physical capital.

What did the council expect in the decade of the 1960s? Table I combines two tables from the 1962 *Report* and adds the actual outcomes for 1970 to be compared with the columns labeled "1970 illustrative." The word "illustrative" was carefully chosen. That column was "in no sense a prediction of what will actually occur. It shows what would be required to move up to and beyond a 4.5-percent growth rate, giving us a rate of growth of potential for the full decade averaging 4.3 percent a year." The demographic projections were taken as solid. Together with a fairly safe extrapolation of past trends in annual hours worked, they gave an estimate of the hours of work available in 1970 at full potential (i.e., 4-percent unemployment). The "illustration" for 1970 was based, quite naturally and without any foolish implied promise, on the hypothetical achievement of 4-percent unemployment in that year. Then, as the *Report* said, "It is a matter of arithmetic that a 3-percent yearly increase in man-hour productivity would be needed if the annual growth of potential GNP is to average 4.3 percent over the decade."

You can't argue with arithmetic. But why choose 4.3 percent as the annual growth of potential to which the rest of the story can be anchored? In 1954–60, according to Okun's estimates, the full-employment supply of hours had grown at 0.9 percent a year and potential output per hour at 2.6 percent, to add up to the canonical potential growth rate of 3.5 percent a year. In the 1970s, the supply of hours was expected to accelerate to 1.2 percent annually. So the "illustration" boils down to a growth of 3.0 percent a year in productivity at full employment. That number, in turn, had to pass two consistency tests. First it had to correspond with what would now be called a growth-accounting framework. That is, it had to make sense in terms of a projection of plausible capital expenditures along a path that returned to full employment by 1970, with a little help from investment incentives already mentioned. And, second, it had to look reasonable in terms of common sense and the recent past. The figure of 3.0 percent growth in potential productivity seemed to fill the requirements. It was a small but significant acceleration over 1954–60, but nowhere near the 3.8 percent growth rate of 1947–54, which seemed to us to depend too much on the catch up of technological progress and capital stock after the war to be reproducible. I note with some amusement that the population forecast was high by 9 million souls, or 4-½ percent; the Census demographers did not know that the baby boom was due to end in the 1960s. Of course, that should not account for the *Report*'s small overpredic-

Table I   Percentage change per year

	Item	*Unit*	*1947*	*1954*	*1960*
Output	GNP	billions of 1961 dollars	325	422	511
	Potential GNP	billions of 1961 dollars	325	441	542
Population		millions	144	162	181
Labor input					
	Labor force	millions	61.8	67.8	73.1
	Employment	millions	59.4	64.2	69.2
	Potential employment	millions	95.4	65.1	70.2
	Hours	billions of hours	129.6	132.9	139.7
	Potential hours	billions of hours	129.6	135.4	143.1
GNP per capita		1961 dollars	2255	2599	2828
Productivity					
	GNP per worker	1961 dollars	5470	6573	7386
	Potential GNP per worker	1961 dollars	5470	6768	7718
	GNP per worker	1961 dollars per hour	2.51	3.18	3.66

1970 illustrative	1970 actual	1947–54	1954–60	1947–60	1960–70 illustrative	1960–70 actual
825	745	3.8	3.2	3.5	4.9	3.8
825	(767)	4.4	3.5	4.0	4.3	
214	205	1.7	1.8	1.8	1.9	1.3
87.1	85.9	1.3	1.3	1.3	1.8	1.6
83.5	81.8	1.1	1.3	1.2	1.9	1.7
83.7	82.5	1.3	1.3	1.3	1.8	1.6
162	159.2	0.4	0.8	0.6	1.5	1.3
162		0.6	0.9	0.8	1.2	
3858	3638	2.0	1.4	1.8	3.2	2.6
9868	9108	2.7	2.0	2.3	2.9	2.1
9868	(9297)	3.1	2.2	2.7	2.5	
5.09	4.68	3.4	2.4	2.9	3.4	2.5

tion of the 1970 labor force, all of whose potential members were already alive in 1960. There is some ambiguity in the *Report* about its labor-force projection. In effect, however, the council anticipated a small drop in the overall participation rate, despite a rise in the participation of women. As we know, male participation did fall, but the surge in female participation pushed the overall rate up by more than a percentage point. How, then, did we manage to underpredict the participation rate but overpredict the labor force? The only reconciliation I can think of is that we were somehow working with an overprojection of the 14-and-over population for 1970; there may have been revisions to the 1960 benchmarks when the census of that year was finally tabulated. Whatever the source of the error, hindsight would reduce the council's projected potential growth rate by a little over a tenth of a percentage point a year on this count alone.

The trend reduction in hours worked seems to have proceeded a bit more slowly than the half a percent a year we expected, by just about enough to offset the opposite error in the labor force. The result was that, by 1970, the council's illustrative figure for the supply of hours at 4-percent unemployment was just about on the nose.

The big difference, of course, was in productivity. As the table shows, actual GNP per hour in 1970 fell 40 (1961) cents, or 8 percent, short of the council's illustrative figure. That comparison, however, is based on the actual GNP for 1970 whereas the council was assuming that 1970 would be a year of achieved potential. So an adjustment is required, and thereby hangs a tale.

There is little doubt about how the Heller council would have made this adjustment. The recorded unemployment rate for 1970 was 4.9 percent. The original version of Okun's Law—which is surely what we would have used in 1960—can be invoked to adjust the 1970 actual to 4-

percent unemployment. By that calculation, real GNP would have been almost 3 percent higher than $745 billion, therefore about $767 billion in 1961 prices. This is some 7-½ percent less than the illustrative projection of $825 billion, a shortfall of nearly three-quarters of a percentage point a year. By our rules of thumb, about 1.2 points of the 3-percent gap would have represented cyclical productivity shortfall, with the rest coming from increased labor force, increased employment, and increased hours. Adding that 1.2 percent to recorded hourly productivity in 1970 gives $4.74 and leaves a shortfall of some 7 percent from the council's projection of productivity at full employment. By this calculation, potential GNP per hour grew at 2.3 percent a year between 1960 and 1970, well short of the "illustrative" 3.0 percent a year. Since some students of the "productivity slowdown of the 1970s" date it from 1965, there is no surprise in its showing up here.

This rough calculation can be checked against the standards of later research. For example, Perry[5] puts potential GNP at $775 billion in 1961. In the case of Nordhaus[6] it is not so easy to say; he does not give an explicit estimate for 1970 and one has to be reconstructed. He does give an estimate for GNP in 1972 at 4-percent unemployment; this translates back to $782 billion in 1970 if the potential growth rate between 1970 and 1972 is put at 4 percent annually, and to $790 billion at an intervening growth rate of 3-½ percent. On the other hand, a reestimation of Nordhaus's aggregative equation for "normal" GNP and direct use of it for 1970 suggests the lower figure of $762 billion at the conventional 4-percent unemployment rate. As one more example, the current DRI estimate of potential out-

5. Perry, *Brookings Papers on Economic Activity*, vol. 3, 1971, p. 554.
6. Nordhaus, *Brookings Papers on Economic Activity*, vol. 3, 1972.

put for 1970 is $775 billion at 4-½ percent unemployment. This would translate into something near $785 billion at 4-percent unemployment.

By any reckoning, then, the council's "illustrative" projection of economic growth in the 1960s was overoptimistic by at least half a percent a year and perhaps by as much as three-quarters of a percent a year. All of this error can be attributed to an overestimate of the coming increase in productivity.

I have already promised not to repeat the standard account-for-the-productivity-slowdown exercise. At this juncture, however, I do want to comment on one important element of the conventional wisdom. A moment ago, for comparative purposes, I recorded estimates made by Perry, Nordhaus, and DRI of GNP at 4-percent unemployment in 1970. Neither Perry nor DRI would accept that figure as a valid measurement of "potential output." Both would argue that the unemployment rate associated with "full potential" in 1970 was higher than 4 percent, and therefore potential output was lower than the real GNP associated with 4-percent unemployment. Both rest this conclusion on a change in the age–sex composition of the labor force that puts greater weight on demographic groups, i.e., youth and women, that "normally" experience higher unemployment rates than adult males. DRI would make a simple correction: The unemployment rate associated with potential output was 4-½ percent in 1970, and about 5-½ percent currently. Perry has a more complicated analysis, with potential output tied to a constant "weighted" unemployment rate. (Nordhaus, by the way, is mute on this point.)

The demographic story does not end there. Most, perhaps all, of the account-for-the-slowdown exercises explain a nonnegligible fraction of the deceleration in the productivity trend by the same "adverse" shift in the demographic composition of employment. Even if output per "weighted" hour had continued to grow at the same old rate, conventionally-measured output per hour would slow down because a larger fraction of the hours were worked by low-productivity demographic groups in 1970 than in 1960.

It is startling, even disconcerting, to observe that neither the *Report* nor the March 6 *Statement* pays any serious attention to the changing age–sex composition of the labor force. Very likely the extent of the coming shift was underestimated. As already mentioned, we knew that female participation would rise, but did not realize it would rise so much; I cannot remember whether we thought about age-related questions, but there is internal evidence in the *Report* that at the very least we did not pay much attention to the forthcoming increase in the youth share of the labor force. What is certain is that neither in our analysis of economic growth nor in our treatment of unemployment prospects, stabilization targets, and Phillips-curve questions did we give the demography of the labor force the kind of prominence it would routinely get today. If that was an error, it was not mere inadvertence. There is a deeper issue involved.

The Heller council was from the start enmeshed in the problem of structural unemployment. We were, so to speak, ag'in it. I do not mean that we denied the analytical and practical importance of the various aspects of labor-market experience that are conventionally grouped under the heading. But the only "intellectual" argument we encountered against expansionary fiscal and monetary policy in 1961 was that all or most of the increment in unemployment since the mid-1950s was structural in character. We were told that much of the apparent slack in the economy was illusory, because few of the unemployed were able to fill the sorts of jobs that would be opened up by generalized expansion. Thus our estimate of potential output was too high, and excess-demand inflation was closer than we thought. (In every recession, apparently, the notion surfaces that unemployment is a characteristic of the unemployed, not of the functioning of the economy. The fine points come and go—"kennel dogs," "mismatch," "search"—but the theme stubbornly survives.) The council studied the question very hard at the beginning and sporadically thereafter. (See, for instance, my 1964 Wicksell lectures on "The Nature and Sources of Unemployment in the United States.") We concluded, as I guess everyone remembers, that 4-percent unemployment was still a good benchmark for potential output; we argued that structural unemployment was real, and perhaps remediable by appropriate policies, but that there was no evidence of a rise in its incidence substantial enough to justify a change in our estimate of potential output. Recent research does not suggest we were far wrong; Michael Wachter's series for NAIRU,[7] for instance, puts it at 4.3 percent in 1961 and I might find it in my heart to quibble even at that.

The deeper point I want to make is that the discussion of structural unemployment *at that time* did not emphasize—though it did not ignore—the demographic composition of the labor force. The *Report* puts it this way:

> It has sometimes been suggested that, though a 4-percent unemployment rate was once achievable in the United States with adequate levels of demand, it is no longer a feasible goal because of increasing technological displacement of workers, rapid obsolescence of skills, intractable pockets of depression, and greater numbers of young people swelling the labor force.

The mismatch we discussed related mainly to skills and location (and racial discrimination). Youth was intended as a surrogate for inexperience and lack of training. We

7. Nonaccelerating-inflation rate of unemployment.

would have accepted the notion that a large flow of female reentrants might also generate structural unemployment, but we would have been thinking about experience
and skills there too. In contrast, most of the recent detailed work on the Phillips curve and NAIRU, and on the
labor-input side of potential output, beginning with Perry's
basic paper,[8] rests exclusively on the changing demography. This must be because the data do not permit an
analysis in terms of more directly relevant measures of
labor quality. One does not expect to discover production
processes whose required labor inputs are specified in
terms like so and so many males aged 30–39, so and so
many female teenagers. It would, of course, be directly
relevant if teenagers are "in our culture" more given to
rapid job changes with intervening periods of search; there
is some evidence that such is the case, but I suspect the
stubborn Heller council would have wanted to see if that
behavior would persist in a prolonged period of strong
demand for labor. We will know more about this in another
decade when we will have seen how the labor market responds to a reversal of the demographic shift toward youth.

These are intrinsically interesting issues, but they are particularly important here because they affect the estimation
of potential output in 1970. According to Wachter,
NAIRU rose from 4.3 percent in 1960 to 5.0 percent in
1970 (and 5.5 percent in 1975). If one accepts that conclusion (or Perry's or DRI's), it has the two consequences
mentioned earlier. First, the council's potential numbers
for 1970 must be revised downward to correspond to a
higher unemployment rate. Moreover, the productivity
projection at any level of utilization should be revised
downward to reflect the less favorable composition of
employment. I have no new insight to offer on this line

8. Perry, *Brookings Papers on Economic Activity*, 1970.

of argument. I was a reluctant and less-than-wholehearted convert to it from the beginning, and I have always harbored the subversive notion that productivity inheres more in the job than in the person occupying the job—within limits, of course. In that respect I have been perhaps excessively faithful to the primitive notions of the Heller council. Time will tell; perhaps it has already told.

The next question, inevitably, is whether the productivity shortfall should be attributed to a disappointment in capital investment. On the face of it, one would think not. During the six years 1965–70, business fixed investment averaged almost 10.5 percent of GNP under the combined stimulus of a tight, or even overheated, economy and the investment incentives inaugurated in 1962. I am not certain that the council had expected, or hoped for, more. Our calculations probably presumed a track along which the economy returned to 4-percent unemployment in 1963; in fact, that milestone was reached at the end of 1965. So the early years of the decade probably generated a little less investment than projected, but the difference cannot have been very large.

I want to go a little more closely into the role of plant and equipment investment, if only because it would certainly have been the focus of the Heller council's thinking.

To begin with, there is a conceptual point to be made about the measurement of capital services that I once thought to be new, only to discover that it had been discussed by Peter Clark.[9]

The response of productivity to investment is usually estimated, explicitly or implicitly, from an "intensive production function" in which output per hour is expressed as a function of the capital–labor ratio. In this formulation, the numerator of the capital–labor ratio is

9. P. Clark, *Brookings Papers on Economic Activity*, vol. 2, 1979.

usually measured by the (gross or net) stock, though it has
long been recognized that the tacit assumption of propor-
tionality between stock and flow of services may be invalid.
The denominator of the ratio is usually measured by the
annual total of hours worked. Is this a reasonable way to
measure the capital-intensity of production?

Suppose that the stock of capital is K, and each unit
in the stock operates exactly h_0 hours per year. Then the
input of capital services per year is $h_0 K$. Suppose, for
simplicity, that there are n_1 full-time workers, each of
whom works h_1 hours per year, and n_2 part-time workers,
each of whom works h_2 hours per year. Then the total
input of labor services per year is $h_1 n_1 + h_2 n_2$. Suppose
that every hour worked is worked with the same comple-
ment of capital. This may require part-time workers to
Cox-and-Box, so that an office with two half-time secretaries has only one full-time typewriter. In that case, the
correct measure of capital-intensity is clearly

$$\frac{h_0 K}{h_1 n_1 + h_2 n_2} .$$

So long as h_0 is constant, this is proportional to the ratio
of stock of capital to hours worked, and the customary
formulation is accurate. One could always choose the unit
of time once and for all so that $h_0 = 1$. The simplest story
is that every machine works 24 hours of every day, each
factory is populated by a constant number of workers,
each tending the same number of machines, with individual inhabitants moving in and out on schedule.

Now imagine a different picture. Suppose there is uniform single-shift operation. If a full-time worker works
h_1 hours a year, then each factory operates for h_1 hours
a year. Thus $h_0 = h_1$; when h_1 changes, h_0 must change.
Then the correct measure of capacity is simply

$$\frac{h_1 K}{n_1 h_1 + n_2 h_2} = \frac{K}{n_1 + (h_2/h_1)n_2}.$$

In this case, the correct measure of capital-intensity is capital per full-time equivalent worker, because that is the meaning of the expression $n_1 + (h_2/h_1)n_2$.

There is still another possibility. Suppose each unit of capital has a worker's name on it and operates when and only when that worker is working. An office with one full-time secretary will have one typewriter; an office with two half-time secretaries will produce the same output (and output per hour) as the first, but will require two type-writers. There are such situations, but they are special. One thinks of violins and cowboys' horses, but certainly not buildings. This sounds inefficient and is probably un-realistic, but it is worth mentioning that under this as-sumption the proper measure of capital-intensity is capital per person employed, $k/(n_1 + n_2)$.

In each case, it is output per hour worked that is a func-tion of the appropriate capital-intensity. A difference arises only because there are historical changes in the hours worked by capital and in the relative hours worked by, and relative numbers of, part-time and full-time workers.

According to Clark, the rates of growth of the three measures of labor input in three subperiods were as follows:

	1948–65	1965–73	1973–78
Hours worked	0.96	1.69	1.53
Full-time equivalent employment	0.90	2.55	1.79
Number of employees	1.21	2.44	2.10

Between 1948–65 and 1965–73, the growth of aggregate hours accelerated by 0.73 percent per year. Full-time equivalent employment accelerated by 1.65 percent a year. A capital–labor ratio using the second concept would have grown almost a full percentage point a year more slowly than the more common ratio of capital stock to hours worked. Using the standard elasticity of productivity with respect to capital-intensity—say, 0.3—the alternative calculation would yield a productivity growth rate about 0.3 percentage points a year slower than the more conventional calculation. If the alternative calculation is more nearly right, then the conventional calculation—the one used by the council in 1961—overstates the productivity growth associated with the expected investment path. It is possible that some of the council's excess optimism about 1970 arose from this source.

The only direct information bearing on this point that I have come across will appear in a forthcoming study by Murray Foss. He finds that the average workweek of fixed capital in manufacturing increased at an average annual rate of 0.47 percent between 1929 and 1976. This is in the opposite direction from that implied by the use of full-time equivalent employment instead of hours worked in the measurement of capital intensity. The matter remains moot, however, for two reasons. Foss's data relate only to manufacturing, where multiple-shift work is probably more common than in other sectors. And his evidence bears only on the 1929–76 endpoints, not on subperiods. So this factor remains a possibility, if only that.

This point about the measurement of capital-intensity provides a convenient vehicle for a little further analysis. The basic model I shall use for this purpose is simplicity itself. It is what the Heller council would have used; with some diffidence, I confess that it is still the way I think privately about the path of potential output.

There is an aggregate production function of the form

$$y = e^{gt}k^a$$

where y is potential GNP per hour worked, and k is the

appropriate measure of capital-intensity. For the sake of
the argument, let it be the stock of capital per full-time
equivalent worker. I choose the Cobb–Douglas form only
so that I do not have to worry about the neutrality of
technical progress. The elasticity a is conventionally supposed to be about 0.3. If the labor supply (measured in
full-time equivalent workers, remember) grows expo-
nentially at rate n, if gross investment is a constant fraction s of GNP, and if a fraction d of the capital stock wears
out per unit time, then it is easy to show that the capital-
intensity evolves according to the differential equation

$$dk/dt = sh_1 y - (d + n)k.$$

This is perfectly classical; the only novelty is a factor h_1,
which stands as before for the number of hours worked
(per year, say) by a full-time worker. If h_1 were constant,
then it could be absorbed into the production function
and forgotten. But it is not constant; if Clark's figures are
to be believed, hours worked grew 0.86 percent per year
slower than full-time equivalent employment in 1965–73,
and that must be precisely the rate at which h_1 *fell* during
that same interval. (Notice that between 1948 and 1965,
h_1 *rose* by about a half a percent per year.)

The equation of motion for k can now be written as

$$dk/dt = se^{(g-h)t}k^a - (d + n)k$$

where h is the rate of decline of full-time hours per year.
Left to itself, such an economy approaches a steady state
in which k is proportional to $e^{((g-h)/(1-a))t}$ and y is proportional to $e^{((g-ah)/(1-a))t}$. So $(g - ah)/(1 - a)$ is the "natural
rate of growth of output per hour worked" in this model.
If h were treated as zero, the natural rate of growth of
productivity would be put at the traditional $g/(1 - a)$. The

overstatement is $ah/(1 - a)$. With the numbers used here—$a = 0.3$, $h = 0.86$—this comes to 0.37 percent a year.

The same model can be used to look more closely at the relation between capital investment and productivity advance in the 1960s. As I have already mentioned, business fixed investment averaged almost 10-½ percent of GNP in 1965-70. The comparable average for 1948-65 was about 9-¼ percent. But clearly the "adequacy" of the investment ratio depends on the rate of growth of labor input, n in the notation I have been using. A sudden increase in n will instantaneously reduce the rate of growth of capital-intensity one-for-one unless s rises to compensate. Thus if n goes up by 0.01, *ceteris paribus*, the rate of growth of k will fall by 0.01 and the rate of growth of y will fall by $(0.3)(0.01)$. Again from Clark's figures, the growth of full-time equivalent employment accelerated by 0.0165 in 1965-73 by comparison with 1948-65. The direct affect on productivity is therefore a half a percent per year.

The growth equation also tells us how much the investment ratio must rise to offset an increase in n; the offsetting change in s is just the change in n multiplied by the capital–output ratio. Another measurement issue arises here, this time one about which I have absolutely nothing to say: whether gross or net capital stock or something in between is a more accurate indicator of the flow of capital services. (There is also some question as to whether the stock of inventories ought to be added to fixed capital.) In the 1960s, the gross stock of capital (including inventories) was just under 1-½ times GNP and the net stock (again including inventories) was just a bit smaller than GNP. These capital–output ratios could be written up by a quarter if product originating in housing services and in government were excluded from the denominator to correspond to the exclusion of the stock of houses and government capital from the numerator. The growth of aggregate hours worked accelerated by 0.73 percent in the late 1960s, and the annual growth of full-time equivalent employment picked up by 1.65 percent. The offsetting increase in the investment quota would therefore have been something between 3/4 of a percent and 1-½ percent if hours worked is the appropriate measure of labor input and something between 1-½ percent and 3 percent if full-time equivalent employment is conceptually better. This calculation suggests very strongly that the actual rise of 1-¼ percentage points in the investment quota was at best just enough to keep the productivity trend from deteriorating in the face of accelerated labor-force growth, and might very well have fallen considerably short of what was needed to stay even. There was certainly little or nothing left over to generate the productivity speedup that was needed to make the council's projection come true.

It was, and probably still is, a commonplace of the everyday discussion of macro policy that a rapidly growing supply of labor makes it harder to maintain high employment. After all, the faster the labor force grows, the more jobs have to be created. The Heller council taught otherwise, provided economic policy could be counted on to look after the demand side sensibly. We used to make a more elaborate version of the following argument. Suppose, for simplicity, that private investment demand will, over the long haul, maintain a stock of capital just large enough to drive its marginal product down to some target rate of return. (We would have regarded the target rate of return as subject to the influence of monetary policy; indeed we would have regarded the constructive exercise of that influence to be the main business of monetary policy.) Then it is a straightforward consequence of the model I have been using in the last few pages that the investment quota will be proporational to the rate of growth of the supply of labor. If deviations of aggregate demand from potential are kept small, then, investment will be more buoyant when the labor supply is increasing rapidly. In that sense, maintaining high employment will be easier, not harder. By the way, when I used the word "taught" a moment ago, I meant it literally: I recollect that Tobin and I have independently used this line of thought as an examination question for graduate students. Unfortunately, I cannot remember how well our students did.

In fact, the investment quota did rise in the late 1960s, just not enough, at least not enough to keep the productivity trend from slowing down.

The missing link in this account is an explanation of the failure of investment to rise more sharply than it did. The second half of the 1960s has a lot to answer for, including the burst of excess demand that was the origin of the inflationary wave that still plagues us. But that very excess demand certainly provided an encouraging environment for plant and equipment spending. The investment quota rose, as I have already pointed out. Why not more?

(In discussion, Franco Modigliani pointed out, in effect, that the desired value of investment might have been greater than the amount actually achieved. If there was excess demand, as we all think, some desired expenditures were presumably suppressed. It would take a close look at capacity utilization by industry to come to any judgment. I suppose I tend to assume that the observed investment share is a fair estimate of the desired share, but maybe not.)

Another interesting possibility is that the cost of capital—the target rate of return in my simple example—moved in the wrong direction. A recent study by Richard W. Kopcke of the Federal Reserve Bank of Boston[10] estimates that, whilte the cost of capital services relative to labor

10. W. Kopcke, *New England Economic Review*, May/June 1980.

services was generally falling throughout the postwar
period, the rate of decrease was perceptibly smaller after
1965 than before. As Kopcke tells the story:

> In 1954 a revised income tax code first permitted businesses to
> use accelerated depreciation allowances. . . . In 1962, the service
> lives of producers durable equipment were generally reduced 30
> or 40 percent, and equipment first became eligible for a 7-percent
> investment tax credit. The maximum corporate income tax rate
> was also reduced from 52 percent in the early 1950s to 50 percent
> in 1964 and 48 percent in 1965. By 1965 the contribution of in-
> come tax liabilities to the cost of capital services was 15 percent
> lower than it was in the mid-1950s.
>
> Although equipment service lives were reduced another 20 per-
> cent in 1971 and the investment tax credit was raised to 10 per-
> cent in 1975, inflation has generally raised the tax burden on
> equipment since the late 1960s: in 1978 the contribution of in-
> come tax liabilities to capital costs was almost as high as it was in
> the mid-1950s.

In fact, the low point, according to Kopcke's calculation, was reached in 1964–65 at just about the time that
the Vietnam inflation began to make original-cost depreciation obsolete. The passage continues:

> Because nonresidential structures were generally ineligible for in-
> vestment tax credits, the . . . tax burden decreased less for these
> assets than it did for equipment from the 1950s to the 1960s.
> Moreover, after 1969 structures were no longer eligible for accel-
> erated depreciation allowances, so the rising inflation of the late
> 1960s and 1970s has pushed the tax burden on structures to new
> postwar peaks. In 1978 the contribution of income tax liabilities
> to the user cost of capital for structures was more than 30 percent
> higher than in the 1950s and early 1960s.

Once again, the low point was reached in 1965. It is
mild, but only mild, confirmation of this story that the
ratio of spending on plant to spending on equipment has
been falling since 1965 while the ratio of cost of plant
services to cost of equipment services has been rising,

presumably because the inflation-induced understatement of true depreciation is greater for longer-lived assets.

I said earlier that there is nothing new about supply-side economics and this line of argument, which is entirely in the spirit of the Heller council, is ample proof. One does not have to be outrageously cynical to notice a certain correlation between fervent devotion to supply-side economics and the likelihood of profiting from investment incentives. There is mischievous pleasure to be had in seeing how quickly such devotion evaporates if the suggestion is made that investment incentives could be sharpened without any net transfer to profits, say by going over to a net investment credit—an idea once advocated by the Heller council—or even by sweetening the investment credit and raising the corporate tax rate. The answer is: pretty quickly.

Concluding Remarks

It is easier to summarize these scattered observations than to weave them into a consistent story. The basic fact is that we overestimated thte growth of productivity in the decade of the 1960s by something like 0.7 percent annually. I am willing to explain a little of that by optimism, high spirits, and the belief that a country's reach should exceed its grasp, but by no more than a couple of tenths of a percent a year. So there is at least a half a percent a year to be explained.

We tended to be simple labor-and-capital people. As I have confessed, we may have paid less attention than we should to the changing age–sex composition of the labor force and its effects on both the productivity trend and the definition of full employment. Contemporary research would certainly account for a substantial fraction of the productivity shortfall that way. I am just the tiniest bit unrepentant, but I am prepared to punt at a moment's notice.

On the investment side, I think we may have erred in failing to take account of the relation between full-time hours of labor and full-time hours of capital. The examples I have given to estimate the magnitude of that effect are quite extreme; the true error must have been smaller. I have also drawn attention to the very large increase in the investment quota required to offset the capital-shallowing effect of an acceleration in the supply of labor. There is nothing new in that point, however, and it is hard to believe that we were unaware of the arithmetic, which was explicit in the literature of the time.

That brings me to the last remark I want to make, an observation—well, more of an inference than an observation—that continues to puzzle me. We talked ourselves out of extreme investment pessimism by relying on mechanisms that I can label with their jargon-names: embodiment, putty-clay, learning-by-doing. We expected more from the pickup in investment than we got. Those mechanisms still seem common-sensically real and significant to me. Nevertheless, they have proved to be very elusive. Econometric research seems unable to find them in the sort of data we have; and the productivity history of the 1960s does not suggest that they are very potent. Where did real life go wrong?

Franco Modigliani: Comment

The reader of Solow's paper cannot fail to enjoy and be enriched by his contribution to the intellectual history of that great Heller council and by his account of the reasoning behind the council's love affair with growthsmanship. I have found very instructive both his exposition of the "model" and his interesting criticism thereof. I have but two comments to offer. The first is an elaboration of Solow's remarks on the measurement of the capital–labor ratio; the second, in a more critical vein, takes issue with what I might label Solow's unmitigated Keynesian "effective demand view" of the determinants of the rate of investment.

But first I want to make a passing remark about the issue of the productivity slowdown in the 1960s and 1970s and what it portends for the future. It has become fashionable to be extremely pessimistic for the future, and I myself have tended to share that feeling. But it seems to me that recent events give some small ground for hope. For, even though productivity growth performance in the United States has remained abysmal, things have begun to improve not only in the developing countries but also in the highly developed ones. Countries like Germany, Japan, France, Italy have all had reasonably good performances of late, even if sometimes below the high levels of the past. It is true that these other economies have had for quite a while a productivity growth well above that of the United States. But in the past we have been inclined to account for that differential by the consideration that the other countries were catching up to our position on the technological frontier, which, itself, was moving slowly. But this explanation is becoming less and less relevant and can hardly apply to the most advanced of the advanced countries. It seems to me therefore that the continuation of high productivity growth in some of these countries and the revival in others suggests that some recovery of productivity growth may be in store for us too.

Coming to the measurement of the capital–labor ratio, I found Solow's remarks most useful both in terms of clarifying the appropriate measure and of providing some empirical evidence on the magnitude of the consequences of using the wrong measure. This is a problem to which I have been giving some thought in connection with a joint paper with Jacques Dreze on the effects of using a shorter workweek as a device to alleviate unemployment. An important issue in that connection turns out to be to what extent the reduction in the workweek, keeping total hours worked through greater employment, could cause a reduction in the effective capital–labor ratio.

I completely agree with Solow's criticism of the conventional measures of capital intensity—the ratio of the stock of capital to total hours worked—and with his suggestion that the relevant measure, consistent with customary production functions, is, instead, the ratio of "capital-hours" worked to man-hours worked. The two measures could agree, but only if the workweek of capital remains constant. But this is most unlikely to occur, at least when the standard workweek of labor changes, since we have reason to expect that the two workweeks are, in general, not independent of each other. In particular, suppose that labor-hours decline 10 percent because of a 10-percent decline in standard workweek and no alteration in shifts; then the capital–labor ratio will surely be unchanged, though the standard measure would register a 10-percent increase. Conversely, suppose there is a 10-percent reduction in workweek, as a single shift is shortened by 10 percent; and suppose this is accompanied by a 10-percent expansion in employment, leaving total hours constant. Then, to maintain the effective capital–labor ratio requires a 10-percent expansion of capital.

But, as Solow points out, it may be possible to obtain an index of the correct measure of capital intensity even though we have information only on the behavior of the *stock* of capital and not on *capital-hours* worked, if we know or can make plausible conjectures about the work-week of machines in relation to that of labor. For instance, if the workweek of all capital is the same as the standard full-time labor workweek, then a correct index is provided by the ratio of the capital stock to the number of full-time employees. If, on the other hand, each machine works only with one man (or team) for as many hours as he works, then the correct measure is the ratio of capital to employees.

Since, in the short run, the ratio of workers to full-time equivalent workers is not likely to change significantly, it would still appear that either measure would give a reasonable approximation. But both measures will differ significantly from the conventional total hours to capital measure underlying the council's calculation if there is a substantial decline in the workweek, such as occurred in the relevant period, according to Clark's estimates (although I must confess that I find the size of Clark's estimated decline suprisingly large).

However, the measures proposed by Solow should be used with care, for they basically rely on the assumption that the workweek of machines varies with that of labor. That is certainly a better assumption than assuming a fixed workweek for capital, but it should be scrutinized in any concrete application. For instance, if the workweek were being reduced by large, sudden jumps in order to expand employment, it might be quite possible to reduce the average workweek of machines to a lesser extent—though our analysis of the Belgium case suggested that it would be pretty much impossible to avoid an appreciable decline.

We now come to that part of Solow's paper in which he has been kind enough to leave me some room for disagreeing with him. Several passages in his paper are written as though he still adhered to what I have referred to above as an unmitigated effective demand view—to wit, the view that output depends exclusively on aggregate demand. At any rate, this seems to be the only way to account for his repeated suggestion that the rate of investment can be shifted up or down by a desired amount merely by shifting the investment function up or down. If this were so, then to increase investment one would need only to provide investment incentives. This view appears to be very popular today even among people that one would hardly associate with hard Keynesianism, such as the two candidates of the major parties (and, hence, presumably their advisors). In the case of Solow, this view seems to underly his analysis of the effect of a rapid population growth on employment. It is even more recognizable in his passage dealing with "the failure of investments (in the 1960s) to rise more sharply than it did." According to him:

> The second half of the 1960s has a lot to answer for, including the burst of excess demand that was the origin of the inflationary wave that still plagues us. But that very excess demand certainly provided an encouraging environment for plant and equipment spending. The investment quota rose, as I have already pointed out. Why not more?

What these passages fail to emphasize is that larger investment cannot occur without more savings, and that when there is no slack, as was mostly the case during the excess demand period of the second half of the 1960s, more ex post saving requires less consumption, either private or public. Thus the failure of investment to be higher should not be attributed to a lack of incentives or to a disappointing response to high utilization of capacity, but merely to unwillingness of the consumers and government to consume less for given taxes and/or of government to take tax measures which would have curtailed consumption. Had the investment function shifted up even more, the effect would have presumably been even higher real interest rates (and possibly even higher inflation if monetary policy had failed to offset the resulting higher velocity). But investment would not have been significantly higher, except in the unlikely event that higher interest rates would have significantly reduced consumption.

Similarly, in the case of a more rapidly growing population, we are told that the Heller council thought that this would contribute to higher levels of activity and employment. Why? Because the more rapid growth in the capital stock needed to maintain the capital–labor ratio would raise investment demand, hence, investment and output. This is again thinking in terms of old-time Keynesian effective demand where all you need to do is have more demand and then investment and output will match. In reality, the higher investment could not be forthcoming unless saving would rise (which might occur partially according to life-cycle models); but failure to rise sufficiently would cause a fall in the capital–labor ratio. Under full real-wage flexibility, this would imply a fall in the real-wage rate, but, under some degree of real-wage rigidity, it could readily lead to a rise in unemployment. Thus faster growth of labor could very well cause more rather than less unemployment unless it is assumed that, in its absence, there would have been a large enough slack. If this is the assumption underlying the analysis, it would seem appropriate to spell it out explicitly. But, actually, Solow seems to rule out this possibility by his clause, "If deviation of aggregate demand from potential are kept small . . ."

The reasoning that Solow attributes to the Heller council seems to me to permeate much of the current discussion about policies appropriate to stimulate investment. No one seems to suggest that at present there is in the economy significantly more slack than is consistent with the endeavor to contain and reduce inflation. Yet everybody seems to be proposing investment incentives in order to raise investment. But if an expansion of output is ruled out, we must conclude again that investment could not expand (at least in a closed economy) unless there occurred a simultaneous curtailment in either private or public consumption. Without such a curtailment, the incentives to invest would not raise investment but would only result in a rise in interest rates as needed to prevent actual investment from expanding. In other words, the ultimate effect of the investment incentives would be that of raising the return to capital rather than the intended one of raising investment.

To be sure, the increase in profits and other returns to capital resulting from the incentives could have some effect on consumption. But in what direction? According to one line of conventional wisdom, higher returns on saving lead to reducing current consumption in favor of more saving. But, according to another line, some part of the higher profits will be consumed, raising total consumption. Of course, sophisticates know that either outcome is possible depending on the relative strength of the income and substitution effects. Economists concerned with this issue tend to be strongly polarized in terms of their "prior views" as to whether the substitution effect is likely to predominate, and significantly. But the empirical evidence seems to me to be unclear at best. My own work, and that of my collaborators, keeps coming up with the result that, on balance, consumption would be little changed if not increased. But, while I am prepared to discount this

evidence which may be colored by my "prior," I remain
very skeptical that one can count on that chancy mechanism for a significant expansion in investment.

In an open economy one further channel must be taken
into account. The higher return could attract foreign capital (or reduce capital exports) and, through terms of trade
effect, could lead to some "crowding out" of net exports.
In this way a higher level of investment would be made
possible, even with unchanged domestic saving, by either
tapping foreign saving or increasing the portion of domestic saving devoted to domestic investment. It is again
doubtful that one could get much mileage out of this
mechanism (or that it would be desirable to pay the subsidies to foreign capital). I must conclude, therefore, that
the popular investment incentives are, in fact, unlikely to
bring about a significant expansion of investment all by
themselves. They must be accompanied by measures making room for the additional investments such as higher
taxes and reduced government expenditures. Yet this essential component of a successful program is left in the
dark by the champions of more investments, be it because
of misunderstanding or because it would be manifestly
less popular (though the Republicans seem to be notably
more guilty in this respect than the Democrats!).

But once we are prepared to make room through fiscal
measures, are incentives still needed? If not, are they nonetheless desirable? The answer to the first question is, clearly, that they are not. In a world of perfectly, instantaneously, flexible wages and prices, one could simply rely on
the gap in aggregate demand created by the fall in consumption plus government expenditure to drive down
interest rates, "crowding in" additional investment till
they absorbed the incremental full-employment national
saving. With more realistic sluggish adjustments, it would,
of course, be far better not to rely on "deflation" to make

the lower interest rates consistent with a given money supply (path), but instead to proceed to a one-time addition to the stock of money of appropriate size and appropriately spread over time, as needed, to accommodate the lower velocity accompanying the lower interest rates. To be sure, this policy might be difficult to sell at a time when the monetarist fad seems to have persuaded so many people that an expansionary monetary policy is ipso facto inflationary even if fiscal measures have made room for an expansion of investment. However, I will disregard these fads and concentrate on rational analysis.

The next question then is: if fiscal incentives are not necessary, are they appropriate? Clearly a major difference between the two solutions is one of income distribution. Without incentives, the rate of interest would tend to fall to reflect the lower marginal productivity of capital accompanying a greater capital intensity. The incentive route would permit a maintenance of the initial interest rate by providing a subsidy to span the wedge between that interest rate and the reduced productivity of capital.

Aside from distributional effects, which of the two alternatives is likely to be more "cost-effective" in the sense of making room for a greater expansion of investment for a given reduction in government expenditures and increase in total taxes raised? It is readily seen that the answer depends again basically on whether, on balance, incentives have the effect of reducing or increasing the sum of consumption plus net exports. In the first case, the more effective approach will tend to be through incentives, and in the latter case through monetary policy. The first alternative may well be the more likely, but as indicated earlier, it would be surprising if differences in this respect could prove substantial.

Two other conceivable advantages of the incentive approach deserve mention. First, insofar as incentives succeed in attracting foreign capital, they would contribute to supporting the exchange rate with likely beneficial effects on inflation. (Indeed, such balance-of-payments considerations were among those that led the Heller council to push for the introduction of investment credit.) Second, investment incentives could be targeted to specific types of investments, whereas investment rates would provide a uniform incentive for all forms or use of saving including, for instance, not only housing but also consumer durables. In particular, incentives could be used to offset disincentives to certain types of investments built into our tax system—a consideration of major importance for some supporters.

It follows that 1) if we can say with confidence that for any reason, including tax distortions, certain types of investment would contribute significantly more than others to social welfare even though they have the same private return, and 2) if we can trust the government to correctly identify those segments, then there would be a good case for selective investment incentives. But if these conditions are not satisfied, the alternative approach, possibly accompanied by selective measures to eliminate tax distortion and otherwise discourage certain forms of use of saving, would be just as effective as the incentive approach.

These remarks clearly do not get to the bottom of this rather complex issue which some of Solow's statements gave me a pretext to explore. But I would like to suggest, by way of conclusion, that the question of how to raise the level of investment be analyzed along the lines sketched out above, rather than along the lines that appear to dominate the current debate.

Global Economic Policy in a World of Energy Shortage

Richard N. Cooper

My subject is international coordination of economic policy, a topic in which Walter Heller took an early and active interest as chairman of President Kennedy's Council of Economic Advisers. My main focus will be on the over-all management of world economic activity in the period since 1974, although trade, energy, and balance-of-payments policies will play a part. I chose 1974 as a starting point because of the sharp increase in oil prices that took place in January of that year. It was a dramatic event, probably the largest shock per unit time the world economy has ever seen. In a mere three months, over 12 percent of the value of world exports were sharply redirected.

World economic troubles did not, of course, start with that sharp increase in oil prices. There was great turmoil in foreign exchange markets in the period 1969-73, world shortage of grain leading to sharp price increases in 1972-73, a world economic boom in 1972-73 that pushed up dramatically the prices of minerals and agricultural raw materials, and the Yom Kippur War of October 1973 which led to an oil embargo by Saudi Arabia aimed at the United States and The Netherlands.[1]

1. Even mentioning some of these factors as important macroeconomic events identifies me as "Keynesian," although a rather neoclassical one, because I do not consider monetary magnitudes—however they are defined—as either the first or the last word of macroeconomic problems or policy. They are themselves part of the interwoven economic and political process.

Finally, it is also worth recalling that the world demand for OPEC oil grew steadily and sharply before the price increase in 1974, from 18.8 million barrels a day in 1968 to 23.5 million barrels a day in 1970 to 31 million barrels a day in 1973, the last figure being exceeded since then—slightly—only in 1977.

The Economics of an Oil Price Increase

On January 1, 1974, oil prices were raised from $3.60 a barrel on Saudi marker crude to $9.60 a barrel (it had been as low as $1.35 a barrel as recently as 1970). Exports of OPEC oil amounted to nearly 30 million barrels a day, so this price increase represented a sudden rise in annual payments to the oil-exporting countries of about $66 billion. This sharp increase in prices represented at the same time a consequential worsening of the terms of trade for all oil-importing countries, leading to a loss of real income; a sharp increase in an important price in domestic markets; and a drastic worsening of the balance-of-payments position of oil-importing nations.

In addition to these relatively well-understood effects, there was a "fiscal" effect of the increase in oil prices in view of the fact that OPEC countries could not increase their spending nearly as rapidly as their income had been increased. If there was a fiscal effect, where did the revenue go? Certainly the U.S. government deficit increased sharply in late 1974 and again in 1975. It was said that the increase in this deficit was inflationary. Yet OPEC had, in effect, levied an excise tax on the world's consumers of oil, and the revenues from that tax, instead of being returned directly to the income stream, were devoted largely to the purchase of U.S. Treasury bills and other short-term assets. From an analytical point of view, we should have consolidated the budgets of Saudi Arabia (and some other OPEC countries) and the United States, since Saudi surpluses were devoted partly to the purchase of U.S. government securities. Such a consolidation would show a fiscal surplus in mid-1974, not a growing deficit as was perceived in the United States at that time. Moreover, it is difficult to understand how a U.S. deficit could be inflationary under these circumstances. On the contrary, the overall fiscal impact was strongly contractionary, i.e., it reduced the total demand for domestically produced goods and services. This contractionary impulse gave rise to a fall in output and a decline in employment.

The fall in output was not due exclusively to the fiscal effect. This Keynesian-type contraction was accompanied by—indeed, caused by—a large rise in the relative price of oil, a critical raw material to industry and agriculture. Thus there was also what might be called a "supply-shortage" effect. Starting from a position of competitive equilibrium, a sharp increase in the price of major imported raw material will shift the production frontier downward, reducing output. Moreover, if wages are inflexible downward, it will also lead (on plausible assumptions about factor substitutability) to a decline in employment. Real wages must decline to restore full employment of labor.

Thus the contractionary impetus of the oil price increase represented the combined impact of this supply-shortage effect and the contractionary fiscal effect. The result was to deepen greatly a recession that had probably already started as a result of anti-inflationary policies adopted in 1974 in the major countries, and it led to the deepest and longest world recession since the 1930s.

One can look at this event also from a monetary perspective. Each oil-importing country (and the world) experienced a rise in the money value of its total transactions at the initial volume of transactions, the increase being

being returned (via OPEC members) to financial markets. The rise in value of transactions should increase the demand for money, and this increase in demand would be reinforced by the decline in short-term interest rates which should follow, other things being equal, from the increase in supply of funds coming into financial markets. The increase in demand for money would aggravate the decline in demand for goods and services (other than oil). A once-and-for-all increase in the supply of money was therefore necessary in order to avoid the Keynesian contractionary effects.[2]

The wage settlement process in modern economies further complicates macroeconomic management under the circumstances reigning in 1974. Wage earners demand, either through formal cost-of-living adjustment or through negotiated increases in wages, to recoup real income lost through inflation. Wage earners understandably do not distinguish among the possible sources of price increase. A deterioration in the terms of trade means that real income has been lost to the rest of the world, not merely to profit earners or government, and it requires a decline in the average real income of all residents relative to what it otherwise would be. A deterioration in the terms of trade on the scale implied by the 1974 oil price increase (11 percent) was outside the experience of modern industrial economies during the postwar era.

The failure by wage earners to distinguish between sources of price increase poses an acute dilemma for policy makers. If they fail to take expansionist measures, there will, as noted above, be higher-than-necessary unemploy-

2. For a formal analysis of the impact of supply shortage on the overall market for money and goods and services, see E. S. Phelps, "Commodities Supply Shocks and Full Employment Monetary Policy," *Journal of Money Credit and Banking*, May 1978.

ment—a self-imposed additional penalty to the loss in real income arising from higher oil prices. But if they take expansionary measures, they might unwittingly encourage the attempt of wage earners to recapture lost income through higher money wages. The once-for-all increase in money supply called for was at the *initial* level of money wages. But an increase in the money supply might be misinterpreted as supporting or ratifying increases in money wages, thus feeding a wage–price inflationary spiral. The direct sensitivity of the wage settlement process, through expectations, to actions by the monetary authorities of course varies from country to country and may not be high; but the possible connection is troublesome.

One way out of the dilemma would be to have a tax cut concentrated on personal income. This could at least partially restore real (after tax) wages without raising wage costs, and would stimulate demand at the same time. The suitability of this possibility of course also varies from country to country, since its effectiveness in this context depends on the willingness of wage earners to restrain their demand for higher (pre-tax) money wages.[3]

National Responses to the Oil Price Increase

As can be seen from this all-too-brief sketch, the economic impact of such a sharp oil price increase was very complex. Different national economies responded in different ways. Britain, Italy, and Japan, for example, experienced a wage explosion following the sharp increase in oil prices and other primary product prices (such as sugar), as did

3. I suggested such a tax cut for the United States at President Ford's Conference on Inflation in 1974. Walter Heller made a similar suggestion, but he would have offset the revenue loss by higher taxes elsewhere or by lower expenditures.

several smaller European countries. The United States, in sharp contrast, had only a moderate acceleration of money wage growth, and as a consequence (alone among major industrial countries) experienced a decline in real wages in 1974 and again in 1975. West Germany fell between these extremes.

The economic authorities also responded differently. The United States, West Germany, Japan, and some developing countries (such as Korea) maintained or introduced tight monetary and fiscal policies to contain what was left of the 1972–73 boom and to inhibit inflation. Japan was able to limit its wage explosion to a year, whereas in Britain and Italy it became more endemic.

Several smaller European countries continued to pursue more expansionist measures, and as a consequence aggravated their oil-induced balance-of-payments difficulties. This was also the course followed by most developing countries. By and large, these countries did not experience wage explosions, but they did adjust their fiscal actions so as to "stay on plan" and continue their growth in output and employment, financing the increased fiscal requirements from abroad. Still other developing countries actually increased their rate of expansion, in some instances (e.g., Jamaica, Peru) based on the erroneous assumption that high prevailing export prices for raw materials would remain high. Many countries took a calculated risk that the world recession would be shallow and short. In the event they guessed wrong, but their actions had the salutary effect from a global point of view of sustaining exports from the major industrial countries and thereby cushioning the world recession.

International Cooperation in 1974–76

The need for international cooperation was recognized at once. It ultimately took place under five headings:

energy, trade, finance, macroeconomic coordination, and a new category called north–south economic relations. I will offer a brief summary of the other headings before returning to macroeconomic coordination.

Oil was the immediate problem. The partial embargo, followed by a dramatic increase in price, impressed this on everyone. The prevailing view within the U.S. government and among some economists was that the OPEC cartel would soon collapse and prices would return to something like their 1973 levels. Such collapse could be hastened by solidarity among consumer nations. With this in mind, Secretary of State Henry Kissinger convoked the Washington Energy Conference in February 1974. The conference addressed a range of issues in the energy field, and ultimately led to the creation of the International Energy Agency (IEA), with its emergency oil-sharing plan in case of major disruption (defined as shortfalls in excess of 7 percent) to world oil supplies.

Over time, the IEA took on other responsibilities in the energy field, including forecasting future world energy balances and establishing a broad common framework among member countries[4] for reducing their demand for imported oil. This framework involves the establishment of national "yardsticks" for oil consumption, and close IEA monitoring of national actions taken to keep actual oil imports at or below the yardsticks. The value of this kind of international coordination lies in the fact that all but the very largest countries perceive the world energy environment to be beyond their influence. Each country's actions are therefore guided by actual and expected prices, and it discounts the impact its actions alone may have on

---

4. Ultimately to include all of the industrialized countries except France, which had objected to the formation of a consumer bloc on political grounds. France, however, cooperates with IEA programs through the European community.

the world price of oil. Yet, in a period of oil shortage, this kind of collective myopia could be devastating for all. By acting together, a whole series of *de minimus* impacts turn into something substantial. Since the actions themselves are costly and politically controversial, the sense of equity involved in sharing responsibility among countries helps overcome the political resistance to national action.

Emergency action on energy was the first step. The second, which was more urgent and matured faster, was to ensure that countries did *not* act too quickly to correct their new and large payments deficits. The risk was that countries would take collectively damaging actions in an effort to eliminate their new or enlarged deficits. Yet the underlying global fact was a huge OPEC surplus, and so long as that was present, the simple arithmetic of a closed world economy required corresponding deficits. Two steps were taken to avoid myopic balance-of-payments measures. First, the 24 members of the Organization for Economic Cooperation and Development (OECD) declared in June 1974 "their determination . . . to avoid having recourse to unilateral measures . . . to restrict imports" for a period of one year in the circumstances then prevailing. This pledge was renewed annually until 1980, when it was expanded into a more permanent trade declaration.

In addition, it was necessary to ensure adequate balance-of-payments financing so that countries would not be forced into mutually damaging actions by their inability to finance their payments deficits. This came to be called the "recycling problem." The OPEC surplus ensured that financing equivalent to the deficits was globally available (provided—and it is an important proviso—that the central banks of the world, and most notably the Federal Reserve System, did not take restrictive monetary actions to prevent the decline in short-term interest rates that the sudden emergence of the large OPEC surplus implied[5]). There was much debate at the time over whether the world banking system could handle adequately the large OPEC surpluses (they turned out to be $68 billion in 1974). There were numerous prognostications of inevitable financial collapse. We know now that the banks did handle most of this surplus, that we did not have financial collapse, and that the surplus itself declined much more rapidly than was forecast in 1974, practically disappearing by 1978.[6]

But even with the major part of the recycling problem covered by the private banking system, institutional improvement was necessary for those countries with little or no access to the private market. The Internation Monetary Fund (IMF), therefore, created in 1974 an "oil facility" which borrowed directly from OPEC and other countries in balance-of-payments surplus and re-lent to oil importing developing countries. The magnitudes were not large on a global scale—about $3 billion in the IMF fiscal year 1974–75 and around $4.5 billion in 1975–76. But these sums were crucial to some countries. In addition, the IMF began in 1974 to auction a portion of its gold. The capital gains, amounting to $4.6 billion over the five-year period of sales, were largely allocated to a newly created

5. The investment preferences of OPEC countries in 1974–75 focused heavily on short-term, highly liquid dollar-denominated claims, including U.S. Treasury bills and Eurodollar deposits. This preference, *ceteris paribus*, would lower short-term interest rates. To the extent the Federal Reserve targeted interest rates in framing monetary policy—as it did to some extent—there was a risk that the Federal Reserve would restrict monetary growth in order to prevent the fall in interest rates. The funds to be recycled would thus be withdrawn from the monetary system. In fact, U.S. Treasury bill rates rose to a peak in August 1974 and then fell sharply until May 1975. And, far from pursuing steady monetary growth, the Federal Reserve allowed considerably less monetary growth in 1974 than had taken place in 1973, on all the usual monetary magnitudes.

6. The cumulative OPEC surplus from 1974 through 1978 was $180 billion. This was about half of the prospective cumulative surplus that was frequently mentioned in 1974. To be sure, a part of this smaller cumulative surplus resulted from a recession that was much deeper and longer than most analysts had imagined it would be.

IMF trust fund for special low-interest loans to the most needy developing countries.

The balance-of-payments financing problem was seen to be a continuing one, however, so another product of the 1974 energy conference was the negotiation among OECD countries of a financial support fund, a fund which would recycle funds from financially strong OECD nations to financially weaker ones in amounts up to around $13 billion. Several key senators were hostile to this notion because it imposed financial obligations on the United States as a result of the oil price increase without imposing any financial obligations on OPEC countries. Because of this antipathy, and because by 1977 most of the OECD countries were on the way to mastering their financial difficulties, efforts were switched to negotiating and implementing a supplementary financial facility to augment International Monetary Fund resources by about $10 billion, and which would thus be available for lending to developing as well as to OECD countries.

The fourth area of cooperation was "producer–consumer" dialogue. A dialogue on energy was urged by France as a less confrontational counterpoise to the U.S. notion of close cooperation among consuming countries, and it led to the Conference on International Economic Cooperation (CIEC) under which 27 governmental entities came together in Paris over the period 1975–77 to attempt to negotiate improvements in the international economic system. The OPEC-led developing countries would not accept an international dialogue, much less a negotiation, on energy alone. The agenda was therefore broadened to include financial assets, foreign aid, commodity policy, and a host of other issues. The developing countries hoped to use the "oil weapon" to extract concessions from developing countries on these other issues. The flaw in this strategy was that OPEC countries were basically not prepared to offer assurances on either the price or the supply of oil, and the industrialized countries were therefore not inclined to offer additional concessions in the other areas. CIEC, therefore, produced only modest results beyond the educational value to those who participated in it.

Macroeconomic Coordination

It was recognized, belatedly, that the oil price increase, reinforcing anti-inflation policies, had driven the world into a deep recession and that common action was required to extricate the world economy from that recession. In November 1975 the first of what have become annual economic summit meetings among the world's largest industrial democracies took place in Rambouillet outside of Paris. The communique from the Rambouillet summit reported that "the most urgent task is to assure the recovery of our economies and to reduce the waste of human resources involved in unemployment." Unemployment in all of the major industrialized countries had reached postwar highs in 1975, and in many countries unemployment continued to rise.

In June 1976 the OECD produced its "medium term economic strategy" designed to achieve a steady recovery in the industrial economies without pushing them so hard that anti-inflationary objectives would be seriously threatened. The OECD had been involved in attempting the coordination of macroeconomic policy for nearly 15 years, since 1961. Its predecessor agency had played a similar role within Europe for even longer. As chairman of the Council of Economic Advisers, Walter Heller played a major role in overcoming instinctive bureaucratic resistance within the U.S. government to coordinating anything with foreigners at that time. He recognized early the importance of close collaboration—even if full coordination was not possible—with other industrial countries on the management of macroeconomic policy. With strong U.S. encouragement, Japan was admitted to the OECD a few years later. Through its Economic Policy Committee, the OECD has served as a forum for exchange of information and views on the macroeconomic outlook and on prospective actions in member countries. It was not suitable for close coordination of policies, even if member countries were willing, which they were not. Countries rarely discuss, in Walter Heller's words, "economic policy in the making." But the OECD has occasionally served as a very useful body for establishing a general climate of opinion on the appropriate course for macroeconomic policies.[7]

This work has been given much more public visibility and greater political commitment by the economic summit meetings, attended by heads of government. A second economic summit was held in Puerto Rico in June 1976. The resultant communique was largely self-congratulatory in tone, in part because economic recovery had gotten underway in the United States and several other countries.[8]

7. If length of ministerial communiques can be taken as a reliable guide, coordination of policy within the OECD grew markedly during the 1970s. The annual communique increased from 2 pages in 1972 to 11 pages in 1979. Or was this a sign of growing desperation about global economic management, as if throwing words at the problems might help to solve them? If so, there is some encouragement in the slight decline in the length of 1980's communique.

8. But perhaps also in part because the more complacent Secretary of Treasury Simon had dominated the preparatory work, whereas George Shultz had been engaged from outside government to prepare for the Rambouillet summit.

The World Economic Situation at the End of 1976

The world economic situation in early 1977, three years after the oil shock and at the advent of the Carter administration, was still parlous. Economic recovery from the 1975 lows, while rapid, had proceeded less rapidly than the recovery from previous recessions when allowance is made for the depth of the 1975 recession. By the fall of 1976 world recovery was faltering. Industrial production in Europe and Japan had leveled out or was clearly in the process of leveling out. Britain, Italy, and several small OECD countries were experiencing extremely severe balance-of-payments problems. These, in turn, put severe downward pressure on the exchange rates of their currencies and led to much current popular theorizing about vicious and virtuous circles, running from inflation to exchange rates and back again. Raw material prices had fallen sharply from their exceptional highs in 1973–74. Many countries had accumulated three years of exceptional external debt, with heavy debt service immediately in prospect as grace periods on official loans were expiring. Imports into oil-importing developing countries grew only 4-½ percent during 1976, reflecting foreign exchange constraints that had begun to take a toll on their growth.

By the historical standards of each country, unemployment was high and still rising in most European countries and in Japan. Inflation, while down from the high rates of 1974, was still unacceptably high in most countries—Germany and Japan being the notable exceptions. By 1976 these two countries had reduced their inflation rates to levels close to their historical norms. The United States, Japan, Britain, and Germany had led the world into recession, and their combined current account surplus increased by over $18 billion between 1974 and 1975, thereby worsening the payments deficits of other countries. Part of this swing, however, reduced the surplus of OPEC countries.

There were serious dangers inherent in this situation. Many countries might renounce their external debts and introduce tight exchange controls. The Group of 77 (a coalition of most of the developing countries of the world) called for a formal moratorium on all debt payments. Default or moratorium would have sent reverberations throughout the international banking system, which was still adjusting uncomfortably to the failure of the Herstatt Bank in Germany and the Franklin National Bank in the United States. While, in many respects, the international banking system was much stronger than it had been 45 years earlier, the ghost of 1931 was clearly present. Discussions among central bankers in the Bank for International Settlements had gone partway, but only partway, toward sorting out "lender-of-last-resort" responsibilities in the highly complex international financial system. Loans by the major banks had grown very rapidly during the preceding three years and were raising questions about the adequacy of their capital and the quality of some of their loans. In the United States the comptroller of the currency was suggesting that several major countries should be considered dubious risks.

The dangers were not only economic. Governments attempting to be "responsible" in economic management in the face of serious external constraints risked having the batons of power taken away from them by political opportunists promoting economic nostrums to conceal their questionable political objectives. Because of growing economic hardship, democratically inclined leaders might be forced to choose between ouster from office and resort to authoritarian methods of control. In the face of these kinds of dangers, special support programs were put together for such countries as Egypt (by several Arab OPEC countries), Portugal (by the major industrial countries), and, later, Turkey. But the problem was potentially widespread.

The Locomotive Theory

It was in this context that the "locomotive theory" was advanced: Those countries that did not face serious external constraints and still had ample unutilized capacity should take actions to stimulate the faltering world recovery and thereby relieve the enormous financial pressures bearing on other industrial countries and developing countries alike.[9] Fortunately, the three countries which did not face serious external financial restraints—the United States, Japan, and West Germany—were also the three largest economies of the free world, together accounting for 37 percent of gross world production. Recovery led by these three countries would relieve the financial pressure on other countries and permit—indeed, induce—some modest expansion there. Unemployment could be reduced in Europe. This was especially important in Italy, where communist strength at the polls was high and growing. Export earnings of developing countries could be bolstered sufficiently to sustain their economic growth and to avoid default on their external debts and the probable international financial turmoil that would follow any major default.

It might be noted here that while a number of countries allowed their domestic economic policy to get out of con-

9. The origin of the term "locomotive theory" is unclear. The term seems to have originated in Japan. A plausible hypothesis is this: I gave an interview to the Nihon Keizai Shimbun in the fall of 1975, in which I argued that the United States, Japan, and Germany should become the "engines of growth" of the world economy. "Engines" may well have gone into Japanese and come out into English again as "locomotives."

trol in the period 1974–76, most countries pursued a course of action that was rational in light of the information that was then available to them. Moreover, it turned out to be globally helpful even if it posed subsequent difficulties for the countries in question. They gambled that the world recession would be short and shallow, like previous postwar recessions. In addition, eminent authorities were asserting that OPEC price unity would be short-lived and that the cartel would soon fall apart. The gamble turned out to be wrong on both counts. But the fact that many countries continued to pursue economic growth—borrowing abroad to do it—meant that the world recession was much less deep and prolonged than it might have been. The importance of developing countries as markets is sometimes overlooked. Non-OPEC developing countries now take a quarter of all United States exports, and a fifth of the exports of all OECD countries if intra-Eueopean community trade is excluded.

The new United States administration in 1977 pursued the locomotive theory. President Carter introduced additional economic stimulus at home and tried to persuade Japan and Germany to do the same. Immediately after his inauguration, Vice President Mondale traveled to Europe and Japan with this message, and more formal discussions took place at the London economic summit in May 1977 and at the June ministerial meeting of the OECD. The idea had the support of a number of other countries. But Japan and Germany balked at introducing any expansionary measures—despite the fact that, by mid-1977, industrial production had leveled off in both countries.

The United States went ahead anyway. The net result was some desired expansion of the world economy, including prices of raw materials, but also a sharp reallocation of payments imbalances. The United States developed very large payments deficits in late 1977 and 1978, whereas

Japan and Germany developed very large surpluses. Corresponding pressure was reflected in the exchange markets, with the dollar depreciating sharply both against the yen and against the mark (and those other European currencies closely aligned to the mark). One of the noteworthy advantages of flexible exchange rates is that each country feels directly, through the exchange markets, the consequences of its own domestic economic policies. German and Japanese businessmen were extremely alarmed about the appreciation of the yen and the mark, respectively, and urged their governments to do something to stop it. The currency appreciation made clear that those two large countries could no longer substitute export-led growth for domestic demand. The American public and financial community, by the same token, was concerned about the depreciation of the dollar, but the depreciation also created important new export opportunities for the American business community.[10]

By the winter of 1977–78, the payments imbalances and exchange-rate movements had become sufficiently alarming to many people that by the Bonn economic summit in July 1978 it was possible to strike a package deal under which the United States would ease up on its expansionary policies (there were domestic reasons for doing this as

10. One line of thought asks why the locomotive theory need involve several countries. The United States, acting alone, would have less impact but perhaps enough to make the difference. Moreover, since deficits represent transfers of real resources from the rest of the world, would it not be to U.S. advantage even to have a deficit sufficient to offset the entire OPEC surplus alone? The answer has two parts, not wholly consistent with one another. First, large trade deficits alarm the public and generate public support for protectionist measures, which those who seek import protection are quick to exploit. Second, large deficits lead to a depreciation of the currency, and that (while stimulating exports and making imports less competitive) alarms the public, aggravates inflationary pressures, and (wrongly) conveys the impression both at home and abroad of an absence of economic leadership. Lay opinion has not yet grasped the full implications of floating exchange rates.

well), but Germany and Japan—joined by Britain and France, whose external position had improved substantially by then—would take actions to stimulate their economies. Measures were introduced in Germany and Japan shortly thereafter.

The Bonn summit represents the first successful attempt to coordinate fiscal policies among major countries on a quantitative basis. The Bonn summit called specifically on France to increase its fiscal deficit by one-half percent of GNP, on Japan to take fiscal action to increase its real growth by 1.5 percent points in excess of the previous year, and on Germany to provide fiscal stimulus equivalent to 1 percent of GNP. The summit also endorsed fiscal expansion in Britain and urged more general expansionary measures on Canada and Italy. This attempt was still primitive and halting, but it was effective.[11]

The Bonn summit came too late to avoid some of the avoidable overshooting in payments imbalances and in exchange-rate movements. If coordinated stimulus had begun 15 months earlier, in the spring of 1977, the huge growth in the payments imbalances of the United States, Japan, and Germany could have been mitigated, and the turbulence in exchange markets which so many people around the world found alarming would have been averted or muted. Earlier Japanese expansion also would have avoided some, but not all, of the U.S.-Japanese biltateral trade frictions which bedeviled relations between the two countries during this period.

There has been some criticism of the Bonn summit results, especially in Germany, on the grounds that it contributed to subsequent inflation. In fact, the rise in the

---

11. A year later, the Tokyo summit created an analogous quantitative framework for coordinated action to reduce the demand for imported oil, with followup to be pursued in the IEA.

GNP deflator in Germany remained unchanged from 1978
to 1979 and actually fell in Japan from 4.0 percent in
1978 to 2.0 percent in 1979. In contrast, it rose in the
United States despite the sharp decline in U.S. economic
growth. The bearing of fiscal stimulus on the rate of inflation in periods of high unemployment and low capacity
utilization has been and will continue to be debated extensively. Suffice it to say that I believe the inflationary
pressures in Europe and Japan in 1979 have their origins
elsewhere, especially in oil market developments, driven
mainly by the revolution in Iran. Appreciation of the mark
and the yen helped to reduce inflationary pressure in Germany and Japan during late 1977 and 1978 and, of course,
that source of price stability was lost in 1979.

Economists teach that we should think in terms of
choices among feasible alternatives. If the dangers sketched
above as being manifest at the end of 1976 were real, and
if they were largely averted, the actions taken during 1977–
78 may at least in part be credited. That success must be
set against that part of subsequent acceleration of inflation
that is attributable to U.S. expansionist actions in 1977
and actions of other major countries in 1978. The devils
we see are always more formidable than the devils we
cannot see. But the latter are out there, and the path the
world economy actually took, while certainly not ideal,
may still have been the best one available.

Is International Coordination
of Economic Policy Necessary?

It is difficult enough to manage economic policy satisfactorily within each country. It becomes even more difficult if each country must coordinate with others in framing and executing its policies. The world would be simpler

if this were not necessary. It is, therefore, worth asking under what circumstances genuine improvements will flow from a coordination of international economic policies. Unless such improvements are demonstrable, there is much to be said for allowing each country a high degree of autonomy in matters of economic policy. I see three broad respects in which coordination of policy results in gains for the international community as a whole and presumptively for each of its members.

The first involves the coordination of targets of economic policy. If targets are incompatible, policy actions by countries are bound to be unsuccessful, yet costs may be associated with their pursuit. Examples of potentially incompatible targets involve different views on what an exchange rate between two currencies should be, or the desire of all countries to run trade surpluses, or, more subtly, targets involving trade deficits and surpluses that do not balance out. A less obviously example involves sharply divergent desired growth rates under a liberal trading regime when the underlying structure of demand cannot sustain such divergences, resulting in ever-greater imbalances in payments.

Second, coordination of economic policy may avoid unnecessary costs that arise from cycling around feasible policy targets. A path of target variables that involves overshooting the target will leave a country, on average, further away from its objectives than would a direct approach, and a direct approach is more reasily attainable with some coordination of policy. Moreover, economic adjustment—the movement of real resources from one sector to another—is not, in fact, costlessly reversible, as it is typically portrayed in blackboard renditions of national economies. If major economic variables overshoot their desired values and have to be brought back to them, resources may be moved unnecessarily and avoidable costs are incurred. These costs do not always accrue to the private decision-makers, as when workers are laid off and then rehired.

Sometimes overshooting can be avoided or greatly reduced simply by an exchange of appropriate information among countries on their prospective policies, followed by an adjustment by each country of its actions to take the prospective actions of other countries into account. Monetary and fiscal measures are framed on the basis of forecasts of the near future, and in open economies these forecasts should depend on the macroeconomic policies (as well as other developments) of other countries.

Sometimes avoidance of overshooting requires more active coordination of policy actions, that is, aligning them to some extent. If the national economies are in synchrony, then anticyclical actions must also be synchronized if large imbalances in payments and/or movements in exchange rates are to be avoided. By the same token, however, these actions must be coordinated so that their combined impact does not overshoot the objective. Moreover, some divergence of cyclical movement in national economies is stabilizing for the world economy as a whole and thus is helpful, provided the resulting payments imbalances do not provoke harmful reactions.

The third respect in which international coordination of economic policy can result in general gains is when it improves the cost–benefit calculation that each country faces in determining its own actions. Fiscal policy, for example, may seem to the authorities in a small, open economy to be hardly worthwhile since the import leakages are so high that the residual impact of a given fiscal action on the domestic economy is quite small. The authorities in each one of a group of closely connected national economies may reason in precisely the same way so that no fiscal action is taken, even though, for the countries as a group, it would make sense. Through co-ordination, such a group of countries may "internalize" the leakages and restore fiscal policy to the (collective) position it deserves.[12]

Countries may actually fear the consequences of acting alone, not merely the low advantage of doing so. For a small country in recession, with a floating exchange rate, economic stimulus will generally depreciate the currency, which will raise domestic currency prices of all goods closely related to the foreign trade sector. The country thus confronts an adverse short-run inflation–unemployment tradeoff. This fact will inhibit expansionary action. Its trading partners may find themselves similarly inhibited. By acting in concert, the short-run Phillips curve can be improved for all.

As already noted, energy policy offers an example whereby collective action can improve the future terms of trade. A small country reasons that it cannot influence the world environment in which it trades. It therefore bases its actions on present and expected future energy prices, which are taken to be independent of its own (generally costly) actions. By acting in concert, a group of small countries is able to influence its future terms of trade, so the actions become worthwhile.[13]

12. This phenomenon is discussed more extensively in my Wicksell lectures, *Economic Mobility and National Economic Policy* (Stockholm: Almquist and Wiksell, 1974).

13. There may be a more complex factor at work here. Clearly, expected prices may be higher in the absence of collective action, and that prospect should produce a strong self-interest in oil-conserving measures. However, public opinion tends toward myopia in such matters, weighing present prices heavily and discounting doomsday projections. Hope springs eternal that developments will turn out not all that badly, and costly actions can thereby be avoided. A large part of such hope is the expectation that the United States will somehow solve the problem not only for the United States, but for others as well. This free-rider attitude does not take into account the fact that U.S. public and congressional opinion is increasingly sensitive to what other countries are doing, so Americans are less likely to agree to difficult and costly measures if others are not also seen to be taking comparable actions. A collective framework for action helps to overcome these attitudes.

Energy and Macroeconomic Policy

As we look ahead into the 1980s, macroeconomic policy-makers in the industrialized nations are confronted with a serious dilemma. On past relationships, policies for moderate economic expansion will sooner or later run into a shortage of oil at existing prices. OPEC production cannot be expected to increase above 1979 levels (of nearly 31 million barrels a day) for a number of years. The competing demand for those supplies originating elsewhere, including domestic demand in OPEC countries, will continue to grow. The more rapid is economic growth in the OECD, the sooner an oil crunch will arise. We have had bottlenecks in economic expansion before, but none with such great and pervasive influence over the entire economy. Sharply rising oil prices in response to oil shortage, as we have already seen twice, can bring economic growth to a halt, partly as a result of its direct contractionary impact, discussed above, partly as a result of government monetary and fiscal response to restrain the inflation generated by the oil price increases.

High oil prices are necessary signals to consumers and producers, so they represent part of the solution to emerging oil shortage. But sharp increases in oil prices are part of the economic problem as well. They must be avoided if we are to have steady economic growth during the decade and if we are to have any prospect at all of reducing inflation. I conclude from this brief discussion that during the 1980s an active energy policy is a necessary component of a successful macroeconomic policy. Without government actions to reduce demand for oil that go beyond simply allowing the market to work, macroeconomic management will be continually plagued by the energy problem. Without an active energy policy we will have higher-than-necessary rates of inflation and lower-than-desirable rates of growth.[14] Thus energy policy is necessary to protect rational anti-inflationary and growth policies, not to mention rational foreign policy. In this regard the 1980s poses a very different set of problems from those posed in the 1960s, when I began my tutelage in public policy under Walter Heller.

14. William Nordhaus offers a rough quantification of the gains from an active energy policy in terms of growth and (anti-) inflation in his "Oil and Economic Performance in Industrial Countries," *Brookings Papers on Economic Activity,* 1980, no. 2. See especially Tables 8 and 9.

Anne O. Krueger: Comment

Richard Cooper has, as usual, presented a masterly analysis of the interaction between international economic events and macroeconomic management. Indeed, he has been a major contributor to the analysis of the impact of international economic events, especially the oil price increase. I agree with much of his analysis, and regard it as a fitting tribute to Walter Heller, who was among the first policymakers to recognize the importance of international events in the formulation of macroeconomic policy.

It always falls on the commentator, however, to stress points of less than total agreement. That is what I will do here. I have misgivings pertaining to two particular items in the paper, and two more general comments and reservations about the major conclusions.

Taking the particular items first: Dick, correctly in my judgment, argues that the appropriate macroeconomic reading for 1974–75 should have focused on the consolidated accounts of the OPEC surplus countries and the United States, in whose short-term securities they were investing. Granting that the reduced rate of new lending, as the OPEC surplus fell, should also have been considered in formulating macroeconomic policies in the later 1970s. In itself, such an accounting would have cast doubt on the need for coordinated expansion, a la the locomotive theory, in 1977–78. If OPEC's placing its excess receipts over current account expenditures in American debt instruments was deflationary in 1975, surely OPEC's reduced rate of current account surplus was correspondingly inflationary in later years.

Second, Dick recognizes the need for real wage reductions and other relative price changes that arose out of altered terms of trade in 1974. He nonetheless ascribes the

1977-78 failure of OECD real incomes to grow more rapidly to an inadequate level of aggregate demand. It is at least as plausible, and, I believe, more credible, that it was the failure of real wages to adjust in Western Europe that led to slow growth.[1] On that interpretation, further increases in the German deficit (which already stood at over 3 percent of GNP in 1975 and 1976) would have induced a higher rate of inflation and perhaps a further increase in real wages and even slower growth than was in fact realized.

Turning to the conclusions that emerge, there are two in Dick's paper which are highly interrelated: The first is that coordination of macroeconomic policy among countries is desirable; the second is that conscious energy policy, extending beyond permitting the market to work and even beyond simply using market mechanisms, and including international coordination, will be a necessary part of macroeconomic policy in the 1980s.

If governments were all correctly informed and if policymakers could forecast accurately the impact of their macroeconomic and other policies, one could not question the proposition that coordination would achieve targeted goals with lower cost than would the sum of governments' independent actions. To be sure, if policymakers were so well equipped, there is still a question as to why targets would be needed. But, setting that issue aside, the "ifs" in the statement seem to me to be very large. It can be contended that synchronized actions in all major countries are likely to synchronize cyclical swings (especially if forecasts are wrong). It can certainly be argued that what went wrong in 1973-74 was at least partly the fact that most OECD countries were in the same boom phase of economic activity, contrasted with earlier years in which European,

1. See William Branson and Julio Rotemberg, "International Adjustment with Wage Rigidity," *European Economic Review*, Vol. 13, pp. 309-322, May 1980.

Japanese, and American phases of the cycle partially cushioned each other. Against the possible benefits that might arise if policymakers could correctly forecast both the likely outcome in the absence of policy shifts and the effects of proposed shifts must be balanced the potential costs of coordinated, and therefore bigger, mistakes.

On that account, the record of the 1970s is by no means reassuring; with hindsight, it seems clear that American monetary and fiscal policies in 1977 and 1978 were *too* expansionary; had Germany and Japan followed more expansionary policies, that would at a minimum have accelerated American inflation, and it might have triggered even more of a commodity boom (including oil) than in fact occurred in late 1979 and early 1980.

All that, of course, presumes that the orthodox tools of monetary and fiscal policy can indeed affect the level of output and employment in quantifiable and predictable ways. Again, the mistakes of the 1970s do not give one confidence that policy impacts can be predicted with accuracy. If they cannot, the case for international macroeconomic coordination on degrees of fiscal and monetary expansion or contraction rests on relatively weak foundations.

This leads to consideration of the need for an energy policy which goes beyond permitting the market to work, and even use of market mechanisms (such as an optimal tariff). If one questions the ability of the political process correctly to formulate macroeconomic policy, governments' track records on energy policy are even more suspect. It can be argued that it has been governments' failure to let the market work that has both prolonged (or prevented) the process of adjustment to higher oil prices and encouraged still further increases in them. This is not to say that Platonic wise men might not be able to improve on the workings of the market, but even then there is a question as to why non-price measures, such as rationing, might be called for, aside from the use of white rationing, which is really a price-cum-income-redistribution measure. Given the degree to which energy issues have been politicized over the past decade, I find it difficult to imagine that the outcome of the political process will improve on market outcomes, even though in principle such improvement might be possible. While I fully agree that there are potential and serious dangers to the international economy arising from the possibility of further increases in the real price of oil, I am not certain in my own mind whether those dangers are enhanced or lessened by the creation of international bureaucracies with which to deal with them.

Unions, Economists, Politicians, and Incomes Policy

Lloyd Ulman

When the council decided to set sail in search of incomes policy on a sea of price stability, caution was not exactly thrown to the winds. Walter insisted that the normative criteria which Bob Solow had crafted so meticulously be called guideposts rather than guidelines on the grounds that the latter, however silken, might be mistaken for ties that bind, whereas there is a presumption of open space between one post and the next. President Kennedy initially called them the *council's* guideposts—rather in the spirit which animated soldiers in the First World War when they induced porkers to precede them through mine-fields—a tactic which, as it happened, failed to defuse U.S. Steel. Chapter Four of the 1962 Annual Report listed not one but seventeen separate measures of productivity growth (including four each for the total private and nonagricultural sectors): the volunteer could enlist under the banner of his choice. The origin—and to a considerable extent the object—of the formal exercise could be found in basic steel, an industry whose leaders an illustrious cabinet member, as he assured the President, knew like the palm of

1. The reader is advised that any notions in this piece which he finds sound and well-taken are the product of my collaboration with Robert J. Flanagan of the Graduate School of Business, Stanford University, and David Soskice of University College, Oxford.

his hand. Kermit Gordon, on the other hand, told the press that "it would be irresponsible to suggest a single, simple, tight formula that you can tattoo on your arm. . . ." As the council trooped into its first-ever (and possibly last-ever) meeting with the Economic Policy Committee of the AFL–CIO, Walter murmured words to the effect that attempting to reduce the bargaining power of Meany's minions while assuring them that no harm was intended called for some delicacy. But delicacy, as it turned out, was either lost or overlooked by the servants of the sons of toil. "Plenty of language there," said Stan Ruttenberg approvingly, his eye drawn like a magnet to the single appearance of the word "equity" (which had been inserted at the insistence of the palm-reading cabinet member).

In other countries experimentation was less cautious and had begun earlier. In fact, the case for incomes policy still rests on a triangular structure erected by *The Economist* nearly three decades ago, although it can also claim support from some unlikely and, indeed, unsuspecting new intellectual sources. In postwar industrial societies, it was claimed, the policy desiderata of full employment, price stability, and free collective bargaining form an "uneasy triangle" because no more than two of these conditions can be realized at the same time. Of course the corners will be clipped with the shears of definition: full employment may be taken to imply a politically tolerable level of un-employment; price stability may be read as a politically tolerable rate of inflation; and free collective bargaining is understood to be carried on under various legal restraints which were originally imposed in the customary interests of industrial peace, freedom of association, and (in some places) the protection of neutral bystanders ("third parties"). Even so, a difficult multiple choice quiz is un-avoidable. It may be spelled out obviously in three alterna-tive propositions:

1) If the community wishes to enjoy full employment and free collective bargaining, it can't also have price stability.
2) If the community wishes to enjoy price stability and free collective bargaining, it can't also have full employment.
3) If the community wishes to enjoy full employment and price stability, it can't also have free collective bargaining.

This implicit case for policies of direct wage restraint has generally received stronger support from elected politicians than it has from academic economists. Economists in the Keynesian tradition have tended to accept incomes policy as a price to be paid for high-level employment. But economists who have mounted a vigorous counterrevolution against Keynes and his works have cudgeled this artifact with exceptional vigor, for two main reasons. First, they point out that inflation can occur in the absence of collective bargaining; and second, they deny that collective bargaining can cause inflation (except under certain historically peculiar circumstances). "Wage explosions" and other obvious instances of policy failure they regard simply as the expected outcome of misdiagnosis, if not malpractice: a shot of sulfur and molasses can't be expected to do much for a cardiovascular patient.

Even the Keynesians would deny the assumption lurking behind proposition 3): that it is possible to secure both full employment and price stability, even if free collective bargaining is dispensed with. Keynes himself argued that the rate of money wage and of price inflation depended on the rate of unemployment. This would be true in part because increasing demand would affect "the psychology of the workers and . . . the policies of employers and trade unions."[2] But increasing demand would also turn up shortages (bottlenecks) in certain types of labor (as well as in other inputs), which would raise wages while it would

2. J. M. Keynes, *The General Theory of Employment, Interest and Money* (New York: Harcourt, Brace and Company, 1936), p. 301.

also oblige employers to tap pools of less efficient labor, which would tend to reduce productivity. Hence, unit costs and prices would rise on both counts; and, since money wages would rise less rapidly than prices, increments in aggregate demand would result partly in rising wages and prices and partly in increased employment and output. But Keynes downgraded the role played by bottlenecks, which he regarded as temporary and as exerting more of an inflationary influence early in the upswing than later on. In contrast, he viewed upswings in union bargaining power as generating discontinuous and therefore delayed increases in wage costs which, when they rise relative to expected wage costs, "can be of considerable practical significance." Thus while Keynes can be regarded as the father of the Phillips curve (a paternity which his critics would presumably be disinclined to dispute), his curve was of the rather flat, cost-push variety.

But many economists who followed in the wake of Phillips emphasized "structural" or "demand-pull" (non-institutional) explanations. Those who did so in the United Kingdom (notably Richard Lipsey) could bear in mind that the empirical relationship which Phillips found originated well before British unionism became strong. In the U.S., changes in the composition of the labor force due to the great influx of inexperienced teenagers and women were invoked by George Perry, R. A. Gordon, and others to explain a troublesome phenomenon: the apparent tendency of the economy to become more inflation-prone after the mid-1960s. Emphasis on such supply phenomena did not rule out continued attention to collective bargaining or advocacy of incomes policy, which, according to this view, could indirectly offset some of the inflationary impact of structural change and at least slow down the outward drift of the Phillips curve. Of course, so-called "active labor market policies" were designed to cope

directly with structural problems by producing better and
quicker matches between job requirements and worker
capabilities through the provision of labor market information, training, and relocation subsidies. Moreover, Gösta
Rehn and other Swedish proponents advocated labor
market policies as a superior substitute for incomes
policies in restraining union bargaining power, since, in
principle, they could maintain desired levels of employment at lower levels of aggregate demand and employer
profits. Thus while in principle the two types of policy
may be regarded as complementary, in fact the advocates
of each tended to poach on the other's jurisdiction. And so
emphasis on the role of demographic and other noninstitu-
tional forces in labor markets did tend somewhat to reduce
the relative importance assigned to incomes policy.

If the Keynesians acknowledge that, even in the absence
of collective bargaining, economic policymakers can have
trouble in raising employment levels through expansionist,
monetary-fiscal policies without encountering more inflation, their neoclassical and monetarist opponents go them
one or two better. They have contended that attempts to
increase employment through such measures must result
in ever-accelerating inflation, and, more recently, many of
them would deny that it is possible to increase employment levels at all through monetary policy. For all
practical purposes, they deny the possibility of a stable
semi-inflationary process of employment expansion; and
what Keynesians may read as an upward shifting of a
stable Phillips curve by the operation of exogenous
changes they regard as evidence of instability imparted by
excessive monetary expansion. The earlier and milder
version set forth by Milton Friedman holds that employment can be increased and unemployment reduced by an
increase in money demand and supply, but only as long as
wage earners believe that their own money wages have

been outstripping prices (and, according to a companion argument, other wages), when in fact the reverse must be true if, under this model, employers are to increase their hiring. This delusion (or, in Keynesian parlance, illusion) occurs because workers' expectations about prices and their own real wages are based on past price movements, whereas current prices (believed to be immediately responsive to current rates of change in the money supply) rise more rapidly than past prices (and current wages). But ultimately the higher rate of price inflation will be reflected in a higher rate of money wage inflation: rising quit rates and longer job searches will raise both real wages and unemployment to their original, equilibrium levels in a decidedly contra-Phillips movement. Employment lost can be regained only by still higher rates of increase in the money supply and hence accelerated inflation.

Like radical children of liberal parents, younger followers of Friedman go further in the same direction, denying that monetary expansion can produce even temporary reductions in unemployment. How many times, they would ask, can workers be tricked into accepting real wage cuts, even temporarily, before they learn to respond instantaneously—hence, "rationally"—to monetary expansion (and to the kinds of economic information on which monetary expansions are based) and thus preclude the emergence of gaps between actual and expected prices on which temporary expansions of profit margins, output, and employment are based? The difference between Keynes' money illusion and Friedman's adaptive expectations can be seen in this light as one of degree. Friedman's worker is an economic mirror image of Voltaire's Bourbon: he always learns and he always forgets. Keynes is rebuked by Friedman for ignoring the long run; Friedman is rebuked by the higher rationalists for acknowledging the short run. Keynes had anticipated his critics with a really wise crack about the relevance of the long run; Friedman offered in his own defense the opinion that "you may be able to fool people for a very long time."[3]

Expectations and Incomes Policy

But whether or not this line of argument destroys the case for active monetary policy, it does lend support to a case for incomes policy, however unwittingly. In both of the neoclassical, monetarist models, changes in the supply of money are viewed as the causal agent, which operates by altering individuals' expectations concerning prices and wages. But this theory maintains only that changes in money supply constitute a sufficient condition for changes in such expectations; it does not hold that they constitute a necessary condition as well. It is not precluded that other things can cause expectations to change, and governmental wage and price norms, guidelines, guideposts, guiding lights, etc. may be included among such exogenous determinants. In the superrational, frictionless world assumed by the newer monetarists, if individuals are persuaded that prices and/or the wages of others will rise by a given percentage, they will find it prudent and profitable to raise their own wages by the same percentage. And then the amount of money can increase in the same proportion; and if it does so, the restraint induced by incomes policy need not give way to subsequent wage and price explosions, as monetarists have tended to claim. Monetary policy can thus be recast into a passive or responsive role—which is indeed one reason why central bankers have been partial to incomes policy. Hence, the monetarist models cannot rule out the possibility that incomes policy

3. *Business Week*, November 8, 1976.

may be effective even in an unorganized economy. In fact, the Carter administration defended its own limited and "voluntary" program by claiming that it provided a guiding light for employers in the predominantly large nonunion sector in the American economy. And incomes policy, like monetary policy, may also influence collective bargains by affecting the expectations of individual union members and their leaders and of unionized employers, although collective bargaining is not assigned any distinctive or essential inflationary role in the monetarist models.

Variable Bargaining Intensity

However, if collective bargaining can make a contribution of its own to the inflationary process, the case for incomes policy does not rest solely on its ability to alter expectations, but the difficulty of obtaining and implementing incomes policy under such circumstances is probably increased. In fact, one has to entertain some odd notions about the behavior of both trade unions and monetary authorities in order to view collective bargaining simply as a conduit for inflationary forces. Not only must monetary authority be regarded as highly autonomous, but unions must present a close and constant analog to the profit-maximizing business firm, as far as their bargaining behavior is concerned. If the latter condition indeed holds, variations in the rate of negotiated wage changes can be produced solely by variations in employer resistance to union demands; each party is assumed to be exerting maximum pressure against the other, and variations in the maximum level of employer resistance simply reflect changes in the rate of money supply and aggregate demand. This model of union behavior is fairly standard among academic economists, but its acceptance seems to have been based more on grounds of analytic convenience than of scientific accuracy. Unionists, like business managers, may always prefer more to less, but they seldom experience the same competitive compulsion to uncover potential gain or to pursue it in a cost-efficient manner. It was an illustrious economist (Hicks) who argued that strikes must be regarded as the result of miscalculation or misinformation (since they impose avoidable costs on both sides). His discovery was made almost a half-century ago, but unionists continue to hit the bricks—and many economists tend to treat them as if they do not. (Or, perhaps, as if they enjoy it enough to make up for any net monetary losses involved).

In any event, we might entertain an alternative concept of union behavior—one which relies on a notion accepted as commonplace by those lewd fellows of the baser sort, the practitioners and observers of industrial relations. The notion is that unions may bargain with varying degrees of intensity under different conditions. They will not always fully exploit their potential bargaining power. Potential bargaining power depends on such determinants of employer resistance as unemployment and profits; and it is also determined by maximum levels of compensation, security, health, and safety, and by minimum levels of discomfort for which unionists would be prepared to strike. On the other hand, there are some minimum levels of compensation, etc., and maximum levels of unpleasantness which they would insist on striking for, even when they feel that the chances of winning are less than fifty-fifty. Such thresholds of satisfaction are frequently determined by customary levels of pay, effort, security, etc., and as long as they are below levels which are attainable through maximum exploitation of bargaining power, union negotiators may bargain within a certain zone of discretion. But if these threshold levels are threatened, or if they cease to give satisfaction to a sufficient proportion of the members, or if the leaders become more aggressive for other reasons, then the union's actual bargaining power moves closer to its potential.

A general increase in the militancy of an organized work force could result in increased wage and price inflation. Its effect would be indistinguishable from the effect of an increase in the degree of organization or of collective bargaining coverage in a situation in which it is assumed that unions always bargain at full potential. An increase in the level of unionism is the one circumstance under which monetarists would concede an independent or initiatory role to collective bargaining; it implies an increase in the equilibrium, or "natural," rate of unemployment and hence of the real wage rate. Yet in both cases, actual union bargaining power is increased—in the former, because it rises relative to potential, in the latter because potential power itself is increased by the increase in the degree of monopoly. And of course conditions which stimulate an increase in union membership are also likely to stimulate a rise in militancy on the part of those already organized. (In the U.S. both union membership and strike frequency— which is often taken as an indicator of militancy—have tended to rise in response to declines in the real wage rate and increases in the cost of living.) However, increased militancy can occur alone, as in the obvious case of a labor force which is already completely organized or otherwise covered by collective agreements. The analogy invites one to draw a parallel between the wave of wildcat strikes which rolled over much of continental Western Europe in 1968-71 and the organizing drives on the North American continent in the 1930's. Organization in Canada and the U.S. came partly as a response by workers to the cost-cutting drives—involving increased effort requirements as well as actual wage cuts—with which their employers responded to depression. In Europe, the first serious post-war recessions, in 1966–67, also stimulated cost-cutting in the form of increased "rationalization" which unionized employers could engage in because, although they were parties to wage bargaining conducted at industrywide or even more centralized levels, they typically enjoyed a relatively free hand in determining work rules and production standards in their work places. (The U.K. had always been a great exception, due to the militancy of highly autonomous shop stewards.) Reaction to this later cost-cutting could not always take the form of an increased degree of organization, but it erupted in a spurt of grass-roots militancy on the part of unionized (as well as nonunion) workers, which came to much the same thing.

Bargaining Responses to Economic Changes

Changes in the attitudes of workers and the bargaining pressure exerted by their unions may occur independently of changes in demand and activity because the latter determine only the maximum (or potential) bargaining power of the unions. Therefore, some apparently perverse wage behavior (when occurring in the context of collective bargaining) is not at all inconsistent with this common-place approach to union behavior. This takes in some important developments of the postwar period in general and of recent years in particular. For example, our notion of variable bargaining intensity can accommodate the phenomenon of stagflation—and even what A. P. Lerner once ominously labeled "inflationary depression"—when money wages rise in response to price increases during cyclical downswings. And it can do so without requiring workers to suffer from illusions of one kind or another and also without requiring unemployment to be a purely voluntary phenomenon, as the monetarists do.

Adverse movements in the terms of trade—notably including the oil price increases which began in the 1970s—can also elicit increased militancy from unions seeking to protect real wages from decline or even to maintain accustomed rates of increase in real wages. Such increases in nonlabor costs, which are not promptly recycled and offset by increased product demand, naturally increase employer resistance to union demands and thus reduce the bargaining potential of the unions, but they may also threaten to depress real wages (via rising prices) below levels which workers regard as minimally acceptable. Hence, employee militancy would be increased along with employer resistance. Unless the unions have already been bargaining up to their full potential, adverse movements in the terms of trade need not result in a prompt and offsetting reduction in real wages (or a reduction in their rate of increase). And the effort to maintain real wages helps to generate money-wage inflation along with reduced profits and increased unemployment. A country's collective bargaining system can help to determine the nature of its response to an oil price increase and in general to variations in its terms of trade.

Unions may try to protect the relative income position of their members, as well as real wages. A theory of the international transmission of inflation by Odd Aukrust has dramatized a tendency of wage movements in sectors of the economy which are relatively "sheltered" from international trade (especially construction, various services, and the government) to parallel wage increases which occur in the more open sectors (which in turn are supposed to be responsive to increases in world prices plus their own productivity). Since productivity typically does not increase as rapidly in sheltered sectors as it does in open sectors, prices in the former have to be marked up (to equal the rate of increase in world prices plus the difference between the two sectoral rates of productivity growth). This transmission of wage increases has been cited in an attempt to explain how a small, open economy which maintains balance in its external accounts may nevertheless experience high rates of domestic inflation (or vice versa). In principle, intersectoral transmission can occur in the absence of collective bargaining: if wage increases in the open sector are generated by labor shortages there, employers in the "sheltered" sectors could find themselves obliged to follow suit in an attempt to retain their own labor. In such cases, however, one would expect wages in the sheltered sector to lag behind the others. In practice, the increases tend to occur simultaneously, under centralized or highly coordinated bargaining arrangements. Simultaneous transmission suggests the influence of collective bargaining—and of collective bargaining which reflects the desire of various unions to maintain either relative wages or (especially in the open sectors) accustomed wage–profit relationships. And to the extent that unions in the sheltered sector are 1) content but also 2) determined to have their wage increases reflect variations in the ability to pay of employers in the open sector, the bargaining pressure exerted on their own employers could vary in intensity from one set of negotiations to another. Moreover, if the pace should be set in the sheltered sector (as has sometimes occurred), the relative wage effect works in the reverse direction and can result in equal wage increases in the competitive sector which tend to exceed the "room" allowed by increases in world prices and sectoral productivity, to the detriment of profitability and international competiveness.

Finally, a union may move to protect the job security or to restrict the effort required of its members on the job without abandoning its income targets. As Slichter, Healy, and Livernash noted, "A union may become interested in establishing some make-work rules or practices without diminishing its interest in getting wage increases comparable to those being gained by other unions in the community, the industry, or related industries."[4] Employer resistance may force a certain tradeoff between effort-employment and wages in real terms, but the extra bargaining intensity elicited by the multiplicity of targets could mean still higher costs of settlement. The militancy of British unionism has long been bifurcated along these lines and has accordingly been assigned a generous share of the blame for the country's low levels of productivity and of growth and, therefore, of inflation in the postwar period.

Bargaining Behavior and Political and Social Change

If changes in union bargaining power can occur independently of facilitating changes in unemployment or profits, they may occur in the absence of facilitating changes in real or relative wages or of working conditions as well. Social and political developments are in principle no less qualified to affect union policies and worker attitudes than are economic changes. The latter do so either when various dimensions of compensation threaten to fall or after they have actually fallen below thresholds of acceptability; the former may operate to change these thresholds or to change union policy within the zone of discretion. While the impact of social and political forces on wage movements might prove particularly elusive prey

4. S. H. Slichter, J. J. Healy, and E. R. Livernash, *The Impact of Collective Bargaining on Management* (Washington, D.C.: Brookings Institution, 1960), pp. 337–38.

in the hunt for direct quantification, attempts to quantify the effects of more precisely defined and measured economic variables have hardly accounted for so much of the variation in wage movements as to preclude the influence of phenomena which economists are usually all too eager to cede to the jurisdictions of the political scientists, the sociologists, or even those untouchables, the journalists. So, in a prepositivist spirit, I offer four examples.

The most obvious of these can be subsumed under the category of political influence, where the bargaining behavior of unions (or, less frequently, of management) may be affected by political affiliations or ideological affinities. In France and Italy, where the largest union movements are affiliated with Communist parties, the latter encouraged bargaining militancy and politically inspired strikes early in the postwar period, whereas in the 1970s, the Italian party, wearing a Eurocommunist hat, urged restraint on the unions and even showed some disposition to oppose the national system of wage indexation, as part of a general program of fiscal austerity. (At this writing, the PCI is divided within itself on the trade union issue.) In Great Britain, it has been charged that shop-floor militancy (a national problem and a national pastime) has in some cases been heightened, if not initiated, by politically motivated shop stewards. On the other hand, in most countries where major political parties are identified with official trade union support, their appeals to the electorate contain either hints or promises that these "special relationships" could yield payoffs in the form of effective incomes policies.

Another example is provided by the strong spirit of egalitarianism which has pervaded Europe and, although to a lesser degree, our continent in the postwar period. It seems notably to have affected bargaining in Scandinavia and The Netherlands, where Social Democratic union federations have pushed strongly for compression of wage differentials. For the low-paid workers, customary wage differentials ceased to be acceptable and they have sought to reduce them; for the high-paid, however, customary differentials remained "equitable" and they have sought to protect or restore them. Such half-accepted and half-rejected egalitarianism has contributed to wage drift at plant level and also to increased organization and militancy of salaried employees, especially in the government. The result has sometimes been a number of inflationary whip-sawing or leap-frogging processes, contributing to both "wage–wage" and "wage–salary" movements.

Another relevant source of social change might be described as a reaction against large-scale organizations, manifested by withdrawal of influence and power from virtually all centers of bureaucratic authority. In the area of industrial relations, traditional taboos against strikes have been weakened or eradicated, especially in the public sector where strikes in schools, fire departments, police departments, even hospitals and the corridors of government have ceased to be regarded as shocking occurrences. At the same time, standards of acceptability in relative compensation, security, and social status have been threatened by advances in the blue-collar, private sectors. In consequence of the increased militancy aroused by those advances, the role of wage follower to which tradition, the concept of "sovereignty," and the Aukrust model of wage transmission had consigned the public sector can no longer be taken for granted.

Finally, the drives for self-determination and direct government (as opposed in principle to representative government) have posed a potentially serious challenge to central union organization and bargaining institutions, which, by virtue of their broader economic and political perspectives, have tended to favor more restrained bargaining policies than have smaller organizational units closer to the membership and to individual producing units. The challenge has consisted in movements for "codetermination" and greater—in some cases exclusive—participation in management at all levels and in all major areas of corporate decision-making, as well as in the planning and assignment of work. Such demands have been regarded as a manifestation of boredom and disaffection by a younger, better educated, less insecure, and less cash-hungry generation of workers, as well as simply an attempt to substitute nonpecuniary gratifications on the job for pay, as real income levels have grown. To the extent that such demands have been supported—or "co-opted" (as is increasingly charged)—by management, it is with the hope that increased employee participation will be compensated for by increased productivity (including reduced absentee-ism). The jury is still out, but a note of skepticism might be sounded. In the first place, workers' tastes and prefer-ences naturally differ; not all respond to the clarion call of do-it-ourselves with equal alacrity. On the other hand, cash and security do have a universal appeal; and while past records of growth and employment may have dimin-ished returns to the well-being of workers from these quarters, it is to be expected that a slowdown in growth (not to say stagnation) and rising unemployment would increase the popularity of income and security.

However, increased concern with money and security need not dim the luster of codetermination in European labor circles, because codetermination could be well suited to support both of these objectives, even if that was not precisely what its intellectual designers, on the left and on the right, may have had in mind. Since it would tend to strengthen decision-making at the levels of plant and firm at the expense of more centralized organs, it could strengthen the forces making for wage drift and emulative wage setting in less profitable firms and sectors. And in so doing it would work at cross-purposes with egalitarian wage policies, since workers in more prosperous firms and sectors would be better positioned to concentrate on wage–profit shares. Thus codetermination has been attacked by some old-line Swedish Social Democrats as "institutionalized selfishness." And while it is enterprise management's hope that worker representation on boards of directors will confront workers with the economic realities, it should also provide those representatives with greater opportunities to secure the adoption of job-protective policies—through conventional collective bargaining. The popularity, if not the effectiveness, of this approach has been attested to in various seizures and occupations of establishments which had been slated for liquidation.

Trade Unionism and Monetary Policy

A bout of cost-push inflation induced by an increase in bargaining militancy can occur without any increase in the rates of money supply and aggregate demand when it results in lowered volumes of output and employment. When inflation occurs in the absence of further monetary expansion it is accepted, even by monetarists, as a supply-side phenomenon. The monetary authority is absolved from responsibility, although, in principle, it might have responded more smartly to the supply "shock" by reducing the rate of money supply *pari passu* with the reduction in output. On the other hand, the monetarist economist would hold the monetary authority solely accountable when an inflation is associated with monetary expansion (in excess of productivity gains). So a distinction seems to be drawn between the fisherman who fails to reel in and the fisherman who presides over a certain amount of un-reeling in response to a tug on the line. It might strike many of us as unreasonable to pin all the blame on the poor fish in the first situation and on the poor fisherman in the second (especially if the catch is of fair size). The unreal assumption concerning the behavior of the mone-tary authority, to which I have alluded above, is that its behavior is autonomous. That assumption, to be sure, is not so popular now, since monetarists frequently criticize the authorities for being all too responsive to outside pressures. In any event, it is pertinent here to mention two sources of pressure for expansionist demand management which can be traced back to trade unionism and collective bargaining.

The first (and most blatant) of these consists of various forms of "direct action," including strikes—official or wildcat—and even occupations which involve establish-ments threatened with closing. These frequently occur in the context of collective bargaining; but, as in the case of strikes for more conventional objectives in sec-tors strongly affecting the public "health or safety," union pressure is felt primarily by public authority. This type of activity may even constitute an extraparlia-mentary channel for influencing public policy, including ultimately demand management, by raising the threat of civic unrest; it has been so employed in Italy and France on occasion.

For the most part, however, trade union pressures on economic policymaking have been generated through conventional political channels. Such pressures may arise out of divergences between the macro-employment ob-jectives arising implicitly out of the specific employment targets of the various unions and the macro targets of one or more of the major political parties or coalitions in the country. Three cases may be distinguished:

1) where union targets are *more* ambitious than the targets of their traditional political allies (who are the Social Democrats in northern European countries and Socialists and Communists in France and Italy) and, it may be presumed, than the employment targets of their more conservative opponents;

2) where union targets are *less* ambitious than the targets of their political allies but *more* ambitious than those of their political opponents; and

3) where union targets are *less* ambitious than the targets of political foes and friends alike.

In case 1), the expansionist pressure which may be exerted on policy depends on the leverage which the unions can exert on parties which they have traditionally supported—financially, organizationally, ideologically—and which indeed unionists often regard as the political arm of the broader "labor movement" of which the trade unions form the "industrial" component. If the unions can influence these political parties either to raise their own employment objectives or to adopt more expansionist monetary and fiscal policies than may be consistent with their own stabilization objectives—and especially if those parties are actually in office—one might think of inflation being generated through a "labor movement effect," whereby cost increases generated by the bargaining arm are "validated" by demand increases generated through the political arm.

However, we have already allowed for political influence as one of the determinants of union bargaining policy; and if a political party can persuade the unions to moderate their bargaining policies as a *quid pro quo* for the adoption of a more expansionist employment policy, the labor movement effect need not be produced. Avoidance of the labor movement effect under such circumstances furnishes an obvious example of incomes policy. A less obvious example is produced when unions are persuaded to reduce their employment targets and acquiesce in the adoption of deflationary monetary and fiscal policies; this is likely to occur mainly in response to balance-of-payments crises, especially when one of the agents of persuasion is the International Monetary Fund. But even if no political influence is effectively exerted on union bargaining policy, the labor movement effect can be avoided simply when union pressure for more expansionist policies is overwhelmed by counterpressures to maintain or improve international competitiveness or just to minimize domestic inflation (as in, e.g., the Federal Republic of Germany).

Nevertheless, in most countries and for most of the time, high-level employment has been accorded political primacy over the objective of domestic price stability, and this ordering of priorities makes it necessary to consider those cases 2) and 3) in which political employment targets are set at higher levels than implicit union targets. Why might unions ever put up with comparatively low levels of employment? If their tolerance of unemployment should exceed that of their Socialist, Communist, or, in North American terms, liberal political allies, that difference might reflect a difference between a wider perspective attributed to the labor movement, with its central institutions, and the narrower focus of the component trade union, which is primarily attentive to the distinctive and immediate interests of its own members. To unionists, a macro-employment objective is more instrumental than it is to a political party; it is a way of retaining their particular jobs. Now an increase in costs relative to demand—or a decrease in demand relative to costs—may (although it need not) imply a greater reduction in employment in the nonunion sectors of the work force than in highly unionized sectors. Indeed, an increase in costs relative to demand in sectors where unions owe much of their bargaining strength to demand inelasticity will be reflected (under given conditions of aggregate demand) in a decline in demand relative to costs in nonunion sectors, e.g., school leavers and other actual and potential new entrants to the labor force. And where unions may in this sense "export"—although completely without intention—some of the unemployment resulting from pay increases negotiated in their own jurisdictions, they might be made whole, as it were, by a general (and fairly evenly distributed) increase in money demand which would fall short of reducing unemployment to former levels elsewhere.

This application of the ancient principle of *cui bono* (or whose ox is gored) of course does not imply opposition by unionists to employment targets which may overfulfill their own organizational requirements. In the first place, they would be likely to support such objectives out of political and social conviction—as members of a wider movement; trade unions have frequently lent political support to causes and programs either remote from or even in opposition to their immediate bargaining interests. In addition, certain selfish interests could be served. Thus (under our case 2) unions could be obliged to support groups espousing employment targets more ambitious than their own if the alternative is to risk the implementation of lower targets than their own (through the victory of their political opponents). Moreover, unions would press for more expansionist policies if their own wage targets were unsatisfied at existing (lower) levels of employment and profits and if they believe that they could increase their bargaining power at higher levels of activity. But if neither of these conditions prevail and, especially if it is believed that higher overall levels of employment could be achieved only at the expense of their own real wage targets, union altruism could be put to a stern test.

Yet labor's political allies, especially when in office, are likely to try to get the unions to lower their real wage sights to levels consistent with higher employment targets.

But the bargaining position of these politicians vis a vis the unions is weak when the unions' employment targets are lower than their own. Their position is further weakened when money wages can keep ahead of rising prices, for then the unions could even lose out by a policy which would feature a combination of wage restraint and higher employment. They might implicitly prefer a combination of unemployment and inflation which, when added together, would yield more "discomfort," or "misery," than the amount preferred by the more liberal parties.

The latter could still try to twist the unions' bargaining arm with the prospect of their own electoral defeat by their common opponents, the conservatives. This argument, as we have implied, may be effective if the conservatives are less committed to what used to be known as full employment than the liberals and the unions themselves; but it obviously loses effectiveness if the employment targets of the conservatives are as high as or higher than the union targets (case 3). It may be noted that, in the latter case, conservatives might have to (and, indeed, have had to) bite their doctrinal bullet and join their more interventionist opponents in supporting incomes policy; but the total pressure on the unions to moderate their bargaining power in the interests of reducing inflation or unemployment or increasing international competitiveness and profitability would still be weaker than if (case 2) the employment targets of the unions are higher than those of the conservative party.

Compensated Incomes Policy

Thus under various circumstances, the political pressures exerted on the unions to restrain their bargaining behavior may be less effective than the pressures exerted on the monetary authority to accommodate monetary policy to the wage objectives of the unions and the employment objectives of some or all of the major political parties. Indeed, even when the overall employment and inflation objectives espoused by the union movement are consistent with those held by the elected authorities, the former might still be less favorably disposed than the latter to the adoption of incomes policies. When unions can dispose of their bargaining power to protect or increase real (or relative) wages, incomes policy cannot operate simply through persuading unionists to lower their expectations of prices or money wages—the role it might usefully play even in the absence of collective bargaining. Now the task of incomes policy may have to include persuading unions to accept reduction in their actual bargaining power in real terms, which could incidentally include accepting reductions in real wage levels. Thus the degree of restraint on collective bargaining required to achieve even shared macroeconomic objectives would be regarded as a more serious deprivation by unionists than by the rest of the community. In that case, unionists might regard themselves as better off with more inflation and/or unemployment and greater freedom to negotiate (and strike) than they would with lower levels of "discomfort" and more bargaining restraint.

Governments may then try to secure more bargaining restraint by resorting to methods of compulsion or compensation, or both in combination. Where the traditional commitment of unions to the method of collective bargaining is weak and bargaining institutions are underdeveloped, and where governments are "strong" in the sense of being relatively immune to pressures emanating from the trade union constituencies, it may be possible to secure the requisite increase in bargaining restraint solely by government fiat, or mandatory controls. (At certain times, these conditions seem to have been approximated in

France—where there have been a divided and politically oriented union movement, sketchy bargaining arrangements, and a conservatively dominated central government with an autonomous and policy-determining civil service.) But generally compulsion is resorted to in order to protect a general consensus—to restrain the odd rogue elephant, as the British put it—and at least tacit assent by the union movement may be required before official control can be imposed. And so compensatory devices have been proposed or actually resorted to in order to induce unions to reduce, or accept reductions in, their bargaining leverage or their desired level of employment.

Compensation may be directed to individual wage earners and also to the organizations to which they may belong. Compensation schemes to benefit individuals abound; necessity has mothered a multitude of inventions. But we may ruthlessly classify them according to the following four objectives:

1) maintaining (in whole or in part) real income—as through reduction in income or excise taxes, indexation of tax brackets or of pre-tax wages to consumer prices, or price controls;

2) changing relative incomes in favor of the low paid, by exempting the latter from wage restraints or by requiring permissible wage increases to vary inversely with wage levels and with salaries as well;

3) substituting nonpecuniary gains for wage income foregone—as through various forms of worker participation in management or in the ownership of enterprises;

4) assuring the realization of the employment objectives in furtherance of which wage and bargaining restraint has been sought and obtained, as by making support of the latter contingent on the adoption of general or specific employment-oriented policies. (For the unions to live meanly, the authorities must live dangerously: there must be specific performance under the social contract.)

However, it is highly unlikely that these objectives would, in fact, be realized sufficiently for most union members to regard themselves as completely compensated for losses suffered or gains foregone through restraint on collective bargaining. Maintenance of real income might be precluded by the requirements of macroeconomic policy. Increases in relative income for some imply relative losses for others; and what may be nonpecuniary meat for some (e.g., the opportunity to demonstrate initiative or exercise authority) may be nonpecuniary poison for others (e.g., shouldering responsibility, and putting one's mind where one's hands are). The realization of an overall employment objective—even if it is confined to full employment of union members—is less important to some members (who may be protected by seniority status or negotiated compensatory arrangements) than to others.

When individual compensation is incomplete and acceptable levels of membership satisfaction cannot be talked down to policy-constrained levels, the institutional fabric of unionism comes under strain. Compliance with incomes policy requires stronger central institutions, but membership dissatisfaction makes for loss of institutional influence and for decentralization. Moreover, if compensatory policies could deliver equivalent gains to workers, net of their union dues, the unions would still suffer loss of membership support—and quite possibly of membership. No matter that the compensation is premised on the existence of a collective bargaining alternative or that it was produced by political bargaining by the union movement with the political authorities. The latter may walk off with the credit for gains that have been negotiated by remote, centralized union organizations and that are shared by members and nonmembers alike. The unions are faced with a new free-rider (public good) problem, with the government substituting for the nonunion employer who keeps unionism at bay by a deterrent wage policy. (In the United States that problem is exacerbated by the em-

ployers themselves who regard nonunion status as more of
a live alternative than it is regarded abroad.)

   Economists who appreciate the desirability of compensation to individual wage earners, including union members,
nevertheless tend to denigrate the impairment of institutional function. The latter might be considered as an
example of technological obsolescence, and union
opponents of incomes policy might be viewed as so many
social Luddites. But this view overly discounts the significance of the adversary process by which pay and other
conditions of employment are typically determined under
collective bargaining. To unionists the adversary process
itself has been a source of utility. To the individual whom
Slichter referred to as "the average and subaverage man,
the wage earner who cannot expect to advance by unusual
skill, knowledge, or exertion,"[5] collective bargaining offers
an alternative to managerial paternalism as well as an
instrument of market power. The bargaining adversary is
not necessarily the capitalist but the manager, who survives
when capitalism gives way to government enterprise or
when the latter expands alongside the former. And the
manager need not be an enterprise manager; a manager of
the economy would qualify when his activities include the
determination of pay. Indeed, in the latter case, the adversary is likely to be regarded with a particular distrust
which the average and subaverage unionist seems to reserve
for the "intellectual" who dispenses paternalism of the
higher order. This problem is probably more acute in the
U.S. than in Europe, where political activity has traditionally offered a stronger alternative to collective bargaining
to the unions—and, personally, to their leaders—and where
loss of bargaining autonomy might impose a lower cost on

5. S. H. Slichter, "The Current Labor Policies of American Industries,"
Quarterly Journal of Engineers, May 1929.

the union movement relative to the social cost it imposes on the entire community. But European unions have suffered loss of membership and influence as the result of compliance with incomes policies, and they have asserted their bargaining personalities at the expense of political and ideological ties in the course of the past two decades.

Therefore, the unions may seek to include measures of *institutional protection* in the social contract, to make up for loss of influence and authority which they may suffer as a result of both the bargaining restraints which they accept and the compensatory measures which they can negotiate for their members. Institutional protection might include governmental support for policies designed to increase "union security"; this occurred in the U.S. during the Second World War, when American unions secured "maintenance of membership" and extended the dues checkoff in collective bargaining, which was severely restrained by a system of wage controls and a "no-strike" pledge. Institutional protection may also take the form of repeal or blocking of legislated restraints on union behavior; this occurred in both Britain and The Netherlands in the early 1970s. It may include "members-only" bargaining or demands for certain benefits which accrue only to unions or their members. It may also characterize proposals for worker participation which envision enhanced authority for centralized union institutions, e.g., "outside" union representatives on boards of directors in addition to worker representatives elected by the firm's employees (as proposed by the British Trades Union Congress) or pooled profit-sharing funds administered by the central union institution (as proposed by the union movements in Sweden, Denmark, and Germany).

American unions have thus far been generally cool to codetermination, which they think smacks of the company unionism of the 1920s, because it compromises the integrity of an adversary bargaining relationship. They have expressed a preference for formal tripartite machinery to determine and administer policy. There is some doubt as to how seriously this proposal has been entertained, but some variant of this American wartime model would afford institutional protection in two ways. First, it would salvage some of the adversary relationship by transferring it to the central level of policy determination and administration, where the unions' representatives could lock horns with the management and/or public representatives. They could on occasion deplore publicly what had been conceded privately—a procedure for which precedent is not hard to come by in the annals of grievance arbitration or public sector bargaining. In the second place, a tripartite forum would bestow a sort of employer "recognition" at the top levels which union leaders might hope would counter the strong antiunion sentiment held by employers at the grass roots.

Of course, the protections which such an institutional arrangement might provide for the unions would constitute serious barriers to its adoption. Employers would obviously be unenthusiastic about bargaining over wages on an economywide basis with representatives of a union movement which can claim no more than a quarter of the nonagricultural work force as members. (In fact, the management community was unenthusiastic about joining on the Pay Advisory Committee, which was established in 1979 under the Carter administration's so-called "historic accord" with organized labor, although they did so largely because they preferred a participatory arrangement to a policy designed and administered solely by a government agency, the Council on Wage and Price Stability.) Nor could official economic projections be designed to serve as opening counters in a "big-gun" (i.e., corporatist) bargaining game.

More generally, it has been complained that the greater the need to engage in policy bargaining with the unions, the greater the limitation which is imposed on the autonomy of representative government. Abridgment of governmental autonomy may be regarded as a social cost of compensated incomes policy. This is not to imply that incomes policy furnishes the only occasion for compensation and policy-sharing with private pressure groups; trade union pressure may be less subtle but also less powerful than the influence exerted by other interests; and unions of course receive compensation and protection in the absence of incomes policies. Nevertheless, it may be that the greater the gap between the rates of unemployment-cum-inflation which each side is willing to put up with, and the greater the extent of compensation required to bridge the gap, the greater would be the extent of policy-sharing by the unions. And so our final question arises: Is the economic gain worth the political cost? Quite possibly the reply of a left-of-center government would be different from the reply of a right-of-center-government, even if both happened to share the same macroeconomic targets and were willing to contemplate the same restraints on collective bargaining, on an uncompensated and otherwise cost-free basis. Faced with an either/or choice, the left might swallow the requisite degree of corporatism in order to obtain less discomfort (especially less unemployment); the right might swallow more discomfort (especially more unemployment) to avoid more policy-sharing with the unions.

In practice, the choice between sovereignty and discomfort, while hardly subject to continuous gradation, is not likely to be dichotomous, and a muddy compromise will be struck. The choice could vary from country to country. Under current conditions, the political bargaining power of the unions in any place would obviously be affected by the degree to which the real wage standards and the jobs of their own members are threatened by developments which have tended to depress the demand for their labor and which have impinged on collective bargaining systems in an irregularly timed series of exogenous shocks. These developments have included slowing (or even disappearance) in growth of productivity, sharp increases in energy costs, loss of international competitiveness in traditionally important bargaining jurisdictions, and rapid increases in a variety of officially mandated nonwage costs. The political bargaining power of the unions is determined by their ability to protect or advance the real (and relative) incomes of their members in the face of such developments. And it also depends on the willingness of the members to forego some real wage protection under collective bargaining in order to obtain more employment protection under political bargaining as well as on the authority of the centralized union institutions which must deliver such a tradeoff.

Conclusion

Following the introduction of the Heller council's "Guideposts for Noninflationary Wage and Price Behavior" in 1962, incomes policy has played a recurrent role in American policymaking in the United States, as it had begun earlier to do in Europe. Meanwhile, the academic case against incomes policy hardened with the general counterattack of the monetarists against activist policies directed against unemployment. The position taken in this paper is that 1) incomes policy ought not be rejected *a priori* as inherently ineffective or counterproductive, but that 2) the policy entails social costs which have to be set against potential benefits.

With respect to 1), a useful role may be found for incomes policy: first, in altering the expectations of individuals (to which monetary policy could adapt) and, second, in restraining the bargaining behavior and the political influence of trade unions. In responding to various political and social changes in the postwar era, sometimes independently of changes in labor market conditions, unions vary the intensity with which they exploit their potential bargaining power; in so doing they may exert an inflationary impact which may be analytically indistinguishable from the effect of an increase in the degree of organization or bargaining potential itself (at a given level of exploitation). In addition, unions may create distinctive pressures on the authorities to "validate" negotiated increases by adopting more expansionist monetary-fiscal policies. They may do so by twisting the nearest political arm and pressing their political allies to espouse more ambitious employment objectives, in which case the political arm of a labor movement reinforces its bargaining arm. Alternatively, unions may exert pressure on demand management when their own implicit (or desired) macro-employment targets are lower than those of one or more of the major political parties, while their tolerance of price inflation may be higher (due to their bargaining power over wages).

Yet precisely because incomes policy might play a potentially useful role in reducing the actual bargaining power of the unions over real pay and/or employment, it may fail to gain sufficient support to be effective unless the unions can secure a *quid pro quo* of some sort. Accordingly, the second half of the 1960s witnessed the emergence in Europe of a second generation of incomes policies, which were embedded in wider "social contract" arrangements together with various compensatory features. The latter have included attempts to maintain the real incomes of wage earners by price controls or tax reductions, etc. to increase the relative incomes of the low-paid, to increase nonpecuniary benefits—notably through worker participation schemes—and to afford job protection. But the economic compensation provided by such devices has been incomplete; moreover, incomes policy would involve the impairment of the unions' traditional role of adversary to management, a relationship which they view as alternative to managerial paternalism. Therefore, unions have sought increasingly to include measures of institutional protection designed, in one way or another, to compensate for the loss of membership support (as the result of incomes policy) with increased authority or organizational security. These measures of individual and institutional compensation may be viewed as constituting the social cost of incomes policy, not because they are inherently undesirable in their own right (which may not be the case at all), but because they owe their adoption to the bargaining power (economic and political) of the union movement.

Is this game worth the candle? Those who hold the candle worthless—who claim that government ought not make employment an explicit target of macroeconomic policy and therefore need not (and ought not) meddle in wage determination—would answer unhesitatingly in the negative. But their basic policy position is probably untenable, and, in the end, their case rests on the effectiveness of unembellished demand management in securing politically tolerable levels of unemployment as well as of inflation. For the rest of us, the political (as well as other) costs of both unemployment and inflation must be weighed against the political costs of big-gun bargaining, and the answer (the least unsatisfactory answer) must emerge from the concrete circumstances attending the case at hand.

Tax Policies for the 1980s

Joseph A. Pechman *

We begin the 1980s with the federal tax structure in disrepute and with almost universal demands for tax revision and tax reduction. Some economists and lawyers are arguing that the emphasis on income taxation is misguided and that the income tax should be replaced by a graduated expenditure tax. Increasingly, more and more people are viewing the income tax as an unfair tax because of the increase in effective tax rates resulting from inflation, and there is strong support for adjusting the income tax for increases in the general price level. Business groups are expecting increased depreciation allowances. Relief for dividends, which are subject to both corporation and individual income taxes, is frequently proposed by the academic and business communities. Some congressmen are advocating adoption of a value-added tax combined with offsetting reductions of other taxes. Two-earner married couples are demanding the elimination of the so-called "marriage penalty" under the income tax. Recent and prospective increases in the payroll tax remain unpopular.

*I am grateful to Henry J. Aaron, Robert W. Hartman, James A. Griffin, Calvin A. Johnson, Donald C. Lubick, Joseph J. Minarik, Bruce K. MacLaury, Emil M. Sunley, Stanley S. Surrey, and James W. Wetzler for their comments and suggestions. But none of the views in this paper should be attributed to them or to the trustees or other staff members of the Brookings Institution.

And, even though the "tax expenditure" budget has become a fixture in executive and congressional budget presentations, the list of tax expenditures continues to grow every year and the revenues lost through tax expenditures rise faster than income tax liabilities or direct expenditures.

In addition to these pressures, some are arguing that tax cuts would greatly stimulate work and saving incentives, increase the growth of output and thus more than pay for themselves. A number of politicians have found this "supply response" very appealing and some are using it to justify large tax cuts even if they result in large immediate deficits.

In this paper, I first discuss these divergent strands of thought about tax policy and then present my views on how the tax system should be modified to achieve the nation's economic and equity objectives. It will be evident that I do not share the recent disenchantment of some economists with the principles on which the U.S. tax system is based. I also believe that the supply response to changes in taxation has been grossly exaggerated by its ardent advocates. There is an urgent need for tax reform, but the reform agenda has been seriously distorted in recent discussions of tax policy.

Supply Effects of Taxation

The claim that large tax cuts will pay for themselves is based on the presumption that present tax rates have already impaired incentives to a significant degree and that a reduction in these rates would greatly increase productivity and economic growth. The professional work on this subject is still in a rudimentary stage, but my reading of the evidence is that the potential impact of tax cuts on output and productivity cannot be nearly as large as the extreme proponents of the supply response view are implying.

INVESTMENT

Perhaps the most empirical work on supply responses has been done on the effect of the cost of capital on investment. The enactment of the investment credit and liberalized depreciation during the Kennedy administration was predicated on the assumption that investment responds to reductions in the cost of capital. There was an increase in the ratio of investment to the gross national product in the mid-1960s (see Table I), but even now it is unclear how much of the increase was due to a rise in demand and how much to the reduction in the cost of capital. Some economists have argued that the reduced cost of capital was the major reason for the rise in investment at that time, but other equally reputable economists believe that the demand effect was much more important. Recent econometric analyses of the evidence for that period and for more recent periods have concluded, as one might expect, that both demand and the cost of capital are important.

It should be noted in this connection that, contrary to the impression given by many, gross business fixed investment during the recent past has been high by historical standards. The portion of the gross national product that went to nonresidential fixed investment in the last 15 years was much higher than it was in previous post-World War II years, whether the figures are expressed in current or constant dollars. The average for the decade, 1965–74, easily exceeded the averages for the previous decade and even exceeded those for the immediate postwar decade, when investment was high as a result of war-created shortages. Furthermore, the investment ratio in 1973 and 1974 even

Table I Nonresidential Fixed Investment as a Percent of the Gross National Product in Current and Constant Dollars, 1929, 1946–79

Year	Current dollars	1972 dollars
1929	10.2	11.8
1946	8.0	8.8
1947	9.8	10.4
1948	10.1	10.5
1949	9.4	9.4
1950	9.5	9.4
1951	9.4	8.2
1952	9.0	8.7
1953	9.4	9.1
1954	9.3	9.0
1955	9.6	9.3
1956	10.4	9.7
1957	10.5	9.7
1958	9.3	8.7
1959	9.3	8.7
1960	9.4	9.0
1961	9.0	8.7
1962	9.1	8.9
1963	9.0	8.8
1964	9.4	9.3
1965	10.4	10.3
1966	10.8	10.8
1967	10.3	10.3
1968	10.3	10.3
1969	10.6	10.6
1970	10.2	10.2
1971	9.8	9.8
1972	10.0	10.0
1973	10.4	10.6
1974	10.7	10.7
1975	9.8	9.4
1976	9.7	9.3
1977	10.0	9.6
1978	10.4	10.0
1979	10.8	10.4
Averages		
1947–54	9.5	9.5
1955–64	9.5	9.1
1965–74	10.4	10.4
1975–79	10.1	9.7

Source: Bureau of Economic Analysis.

exceeded the ratio in 1929 when it is measured in current dollars. (It was below the 1929 ratio in constant dollars—as was every year since the end of World War II.) After a drop during the 1975 recession, the investment ratio came back to previous peak levels in 1978 and 1979 (Table I).

Thus there is no evidence that business investment has been lagging in recent years. It is true that capital per worker declined after 1973, but this drop was due to the large increase in the labor force, not to any particular feature of the tax system or to changes in tax policy.

The fact that investment has been high recently does not mean that it should not be higher still. But we should not exaggerate the potential effect of taxes in achieving higher productivity growth through increased investment. Most analysts agree that an increase of one percentage point in the ratio of investment to the gross national product—about $28 billion in 1981—would generate a 0.2 percentage-point increase in the annual rate of productivity growth. Thus even if business taxes were cut by $28 billion a year and the entire tax cut were funnelled into investment, the effect on the growth rate would be modest.

The major constraint on investment in current conditions is the decline in demand resulting from the recession which began early in 1980, a recession generated by restrictive monetary policies adopted to slow what was then a roaring inflation. Based on past experience, a recession reduces investment by 10–15 percent for each year in which the economy is operating significantly below trend. Thus a three-year period of recession and catchup would reduce investment by a third to half a year's worth of investment. I know of no technique, tax or otherwise, that would raise investment by that amount over the next three years. The moral of this story is that the best way to secure adequate investment is to avoid recession; and the best way to avoid recession is to moderate inflation so that it will not be necessary to slow down the economy as a counter-inflation measure.

SAVING

The case for tax incentives to promote saving is that more saving is necessary to provide the resources necessary to increase business investment. However, the evidence on the effect of increasing the rate of return on saving is unsatisfactory. Some economists have made calculations suggesting that the elasticity of saving with respect to the return on saving is fairly high (up to 0.4), but other calculations suggest that the personal saving elasticity is close to zero. The prevailing view is that there is some interest elasticity to saving, but we really don't know what it is.

There is the additional complication that higher private saving may not translate into a higher level of total saving or increased business investment. For one thing, given the larger tax and other advantages accorded to residential construction, much of the additional saving might find its way into the housing sector rather than the business sector. Furthermore, if there is a problem of inadequate business capital formation in the United States, it may be more the result of the uncertainties about the payoff from investment rather than a shortage of saving. The uncertainties have been particularly acute in the recent years of serious inflation and severe recessions. In such circumstances, cuts in income tax rates or the introduction of new tax preferences for saving may have very little payoff. Finally, when the economy is operating at high levels, a sizable surplus in the federal budget offers a more certain method of increasing funds for private investment than would tax cuts or tax preferences.

THE STOCK MARKET

The tax system is a favorite target of criticism whenever the stock market is in trouble. Many analysts on Wall Street argued that the increase in the maximum tax rate on capital gains from 25 to 40 percent for most taxpayers as a result of legislation in 1969 (and to 50 percent for a few taxpayers who were subject to both the maximum tax on earned income and the minimum tax on tax preferences beginning in 1977) caused the stock market to perform badly in the late 1970s. In 1978, they were influential enough to persuade Congress to reduce the tax rates on capital gains to 40 percent of the regular rates, thus reducing the maximum capital gains rate to 28 percent (40 percent of the present maximum marginal tax rate of 70 percent).

It is worth recalling that some wild estimates were made of the expected stock market response to this large reduction in the capital gains tax. Some predicted that the stock market would go up by as much as 40 percent, while others predicted that the number of transactions generating capital gains would triple (and, therefore, there would be no revenue loss from the capital gains tax reduction). Such predictions have, of course, proved wrong. Again, more recent econometric work has confirmed that the early estimates vastly overstated the response of stock prices and capital gains transactions to a reduction in the capital gains rate.

LABOR SUPPLY

A series of econometric studies dating back to the 1960s concluded that the labor supply of prime-age males is not highly sensitive to changes in net earnings, but that the labor supply of wives and other family members does respond to changes in the rewards for working. According to interview studies both in the United States and England, tax rates have little effect on work effort of high-bracket taxpayers and of professional groups. Recent econometric work has confirmed that the labor supply response of supplementary family earners to earnings changes is significant, and the response of prime-age males may be higher than we have believed in the past, although it is still relatively small. The econometrics required to obtain such estimates from available cross-section data are difficult and a lot more work needs to be done to evaluate these new findings. The evidence does suggest that reductions in tax rates for working wives would have a significant supply response (although recent increases in labor force participation of married women can hardly be accelerated very much). However, even using the most generous estimates of the elasticity of total labor supply, it is clear that tax cuts will not raise output enough to pay for themselves.

IMPLICATIONS FOR POLICY

In view of the tenuous nature of the evidence, there is no basis for assuming that reductions in income tax rates—some have proposed as much as 30 percent—will increase incentives and productivity growth by large amounts. The recent decline in the rate of growth of productivity is worrisome, but the problem will not be solved by such a simple expedient as tax reduction. Moreover, in current and foreseeable circumstances, federal tax resources must be carefully husbanded and it would be irresponsible to accept significantly higher deficits in the expectation that higher tax receipts would erase the deficit.

The evidence does suggest that two tax measures would have reasonably good, though not spectacular, payoffs. First, a reduction in the cost of capital either through an increased investment credit or higher depreciation allowances would stimulate investment, which would in the long run result in a modest increase in productivity growth. Second, reductions in the marginal tax rates of married couples might encourage some spouses to work longer hours.

Consumption Taxes

Two types of consumption taxes have been receiving a good deal of prominence in recent discussions of tax policy, though the support for each comes from entirely different quarters. A value-added tax is being discussed by some politicians who are attracted by its large revenue potential and wish to reduce the emphasis now placed on income and payroll taxes. On the other hand, a considerable number of economists and tax lawyers have become intrigued with the possibility of substituting a graduated expenditure tax for the present individual and corporation income taxes. The rationale and consequences of these approaches need to be carefully distinguished. In my view, the adoption of a value-added tax cannot be supported on equity, economic, or administrative grounds. The expenditure tax has more to be said for it, but I believe it is both unwise and impractical to consider making such a radical change in the tax system.

THE VALUE-ADDED TAX

The value-added tax was widely adopted in Europe primarily to replace turnover taxes which were pyramided and distorted business organization. The enactment of the value-added tax in those circumstances was a real reform of the consumption taxes then in use. Here, the value-added tax would be a new tax that would replace income and payroll taxes whose inefficiencies hardly compare to those of the European turnover taxes.

The value-added tax which is under discussion is nothing more than a retail sales tax. The only difference between the two taxes is that the value-added tax is collected as goods move through the production and distribution system, while the sales tax is collected only at the retail or final stage of sales.

A value-added tax would, of course, increase consumer prices by the amount of the tax (assuming an accommodative monetary policy). Even if most of the revenue from the tax were substituted for the payroll tax, the net effect of the change would be to raise the price level since only half of the payroll tax change would reduce the employer taxes which enter into business costs. Any substitution of value-added tax for income tax revenue would increase inflation, as the income taxes do not affect prices to any significant degree while a value-added tax would probably be fully reflected in prices. In the present and foreseeable circumstances, it is irresponsible to contemplate the introduction of such an inflationary tax.

The substitution of a value-added tax for a major part of the income tax would be a regressive step (see Figure 1). The national tax system is only moderately progressive, if at all, because state and local sales and excise taxes and payroll taxes offset the progressivity of the income taxes at the federal and state levels. To justify the enactment of the value-added tax, it would be necessary to argue that a shift in the tax burden from high- to low-income groups is appropriate, a position which few would care openly to defend.

Some have argued that the regressivity of the value-added tax can be offset by tax credits at the lower income levels, but this is not a complete remedy. A credit would make the value-added tax progressive only up to the point where the maximum credit is paid and would place the largest relative tax burden at the point where the credit phases out, usually at incomes between $10,000 and $15,000. Beyond that point, the value-added tax would be regressive. The logic of putting the maximum burden of a new tax on people with incomes of $10,000–$15,000 escapes me. Nor do I see any point in first imposing a tax on low-income recipients and then giving them a credit to offset it.

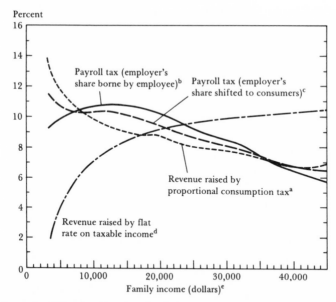

Figure 1 Effective Tax Rates of the Payroll Tax and of Alternative
Metods of Raising the Same Revenue, 1977

Source: Joseph A. Pechman, *Federal Tax Policy* (Brookings Institution,
1977), p. 207.

a. Tax is 11.7 percent for wage earners and 7.9 percent for the self-employed.
Maximum earnings subject to tax are $16,500.

b. Both the employer and the employee portions of the tax are assumed to
be borne by the employee; the self-employment tax by the self-employed.

c. The employer tax is distributed in proportion to consumption by income class; the employee tax and self-employment tax by the employee and
the self-employed, respectively.

d. The tax is applied to taxable income as defined in the income tax law
for 1977.

e. Family income is a comprehensive definition of income, which includes
estimated accrued capital gains.

The enactment of the value-added tax would bring the
federal government into an area that is now one of the
most important sources of state revenue and is also important in many localities. Federal use of the value-added tax
would greatly complicate compliance on the part of

businessmen, since the general form of consumption tax levied at the state–local level is the sales tax and not the value-added tax. Thus most businessmen would be burdened with the problem of complying with two different types of sales taxes, requiring separate sets of records and duplicate procedures for tax collection, payment, and compliance.

The value-added tax is often supported on the ground that it would increase saving, but the net effect as compared to an equal-yield income tax of the type now in effect would be small. If we are serious about increasing the rate of national saving, the easiest way would be to move toward a surplus in the federal budget. The effect of such a policy is demonstrable and would be large; the impact of a value-added tax on saving is speculative and would be small.

I believe that proponents of the value-added tax are really interested in substituting some value-added taxation for the income tax in order to reduce the progressivity of the tax system. This is the real issue and it should not be camouflaged by arguments regarding growth, productivity and investment. In my opinion, the income tax is not oppressive and there is no reason to introduce another regressive tax into the tax system.

THE EXPENDITURE TAX

The expenditure tax is a personal tax levied on individual income less saving. In contrast to the value-added tax, the expenditure tax is designed to be a graduated tax. The idea of the expenditure tax dates back at least to John Stuart Mill. It was promoted without success in this country by Irving Fisher before World War II and in Britain by Nicholas Kaldor in the 1950s. Recently, it has been revived by a group of economists and lawyers who are attracted by a tax which does not apply to saving and does not have many of the problems of taxing income from property that plague the income taxes.

In theory (but probably not in practice), it is possible to approximate the degree of a progression of an income tax by an expenditure tax. Basically, the choice between the income and expenditure taxes is dictated by a value judgment: supporters of the income tax believe that income is a better measure of ability-to-pay than consumption; expenditure tax advocates believe that it is more appropriate to tax what people withdraw from the economic system (consumption) than what people contribute to the system (income).

A basic difference between the income and expenditure taxes is in the time perspective of the two taxes. The perspective of the income tax is relatively short-run—a year or several years (to allow for short-run income fluctuations). Consumption, which is more stable than income, is a better measure of long-term well-being. If there is no tax on saving and no gifts or bequests, the present values of the lifetime expenditures of two people with the same discounted lifetime incomes are the same regardless of when they consume. Advocates of the expenditure tax regard this lifetime perspective as a major advantage because it provides equal treatment for taxpayers with the same endowment (that is, the same present value of lifetime incomes). Supporters of the income tax see no merit in a tax based on endowments rather than on actual outcomes. Moreover, the lifetime perspective in taxation hardly seems appropriate in a world of substantial family instability, economic and political changes, and uncertainty. One inevitable result of the substitution of an expenditure tax for the income tax would be to raise the taxes on younger and older people relative to the taxes of those in middle age who tend to save more. Many people would regard this result, which is an outcome of the endowment or lifetime perspective of the expenditure tax, as a step in exactly the wrong direction.

The expenditure tax would encourage saving more than an equal-yield income tax distributed in the same proportions by income classes. However, since the elasticity of saving with respect to the rate of return is not known, there is no way to predict how much saving would increase if the income tax was replaced by an expenditure tax. It should be added that, even if their rate of saving from current income remained the same, individuals could consume more because of the higher after-tax return on their saving. They would therefore be able to improve their welfare by consuming more in later years or by reallocating their consumption over their lifetimes.

Inflation would be much less of a problem under the expenditure tax than it is under the income tax. In general, there would be no need to adjust the tax *base* for inflation, as consumption would appropriately be measured in current dollars. It might be considered desirable to index the expenditure tax rate brackets and personal exemptions, but this decision would involve the same considerations discussed in connection with indexing the income tax brackets and exemptions (see below).

Under an expenditure tax, taxpayers who save large fractions of their income would be able to accumulate large amounts of wealth over a lifetime. Many, but by no means all, expenditure tax advocates support effective wealth or estate and gift taxes to prevent excessive concentrations of wealth. But the history of transfer taxation in this country and abroad provides little assurance that effective death and gift taxes would be levied to supplement the expenditure tax.

To avoid a reduction in revenues, expenditure tax rates would have to be higher than income tax rates. For example, if an individual is subject to a 50-percent marginal income tax rate and his marginal saving rate is 50 percent of his marginal disposable income, the marginal tax rate on income less saving would have to be 66-2/3 percent to raise the same revenue (assuming saving remains the same). Tax rates on the purchase of housing and consumer durables would be extremely high and would probably be regarded as excessive by most people. (As an alternative, the services provided by houses and durables could be taxed, but few noneconomists could be persuaded to accept taxation of such imputed income.)

The transition from the income tax to an expenditure tax would be troublesome. The retired elderly would not benefit from the exemption for saving, because they draw down assets to finance current consumption. Thus allowances would be needed to avoid taxing accumulations under the expenditure tax that were already taxed under the income tax. Exemption of all accumulated assets at the time an expenditure tax is initiated would leave a big loophole for people with large amounts of accrued capital appreciation that had not been subject to tax, but it would not be easy to make the necessary distinctions in order to prevent wholesale tax avoidance.

Proponents of the expenditure tax often compare the merits of a comprehensive expenditure tax with the income tax as it has actually developed. In fact, most of the eroding features of the income tax could be carried over in one way or another to the expenditure tax. Housing is favorably treated under the income tax and would doubtless be exempt under the expenditure tax. Outlays such as charitable contributions, state and local property and sales taxes, and medical expenses, which are deductible under the income tax, would probably be regarded as equally meritorious under the expenditure tax. The special exemptions for the elderly and the tax credits for child care, energy, and other outlays could play the same role under the expenditure tax as they do under the income tax. Beyond these items, other pressure groups would find good reasons for excluding other personal outlays from the expenditure tax base. (India, which enacted an expenditure tax but never implemented it, provided a deduction for outlays on weddings, for example.) Thus an expenditure tax would be no less immune to erosion than the income tax and, in such circumstances, it loses much of its attractiveness.

Administration and compliance would be easier under the expenditure tax than under the income tax in some respects and more difficult in others. The expenditure tax would eliminate all the problems arising from the use of the realization principle for calculating capital gains and losses and the accounting conventions for depreciation and depletion in arriving at net business profits. On the other hand, changes in cash holdings and personal debts and purchases and dispositions of personal assets (such as jewelry and paintings) would be hard to trace. Although balance sheets are not absolutely essential to administer an expenditure tax, it would be better to have them in order to prevent taxpayers from aribitrarily reporting their asset sales when it was to their advantage. Otherwise, the timing of tax payments would be entirely at the discretion of the taxpayer. Most expenditure tax proponents disregard this problem (some even consider discretionary timing of tax payments a virtue), but it is doubtful that this would be acceptable by the mass of taxpayers who would not have the same opportunities for determining when their tax would be paid.

In summary, the expenditure tax would increase the incentive to save and avoid the problems of adjusting the tax base for inflation. It would probably be subject to the same, or greater, pressures for special treatment that are evident in the income tax. Administration of and compliance with an expenditure tax would be complicated, but the problems would not be insuperable for a country like the United States which has had considerable experience with income taxation. The transition problems in shifting from an income tax to an expenditure tax would be difficult, and the expenditure tax would lend itself to at least as much manipulation to avoid tax as the income tax. The substitution of an expenditure tax for the income tax would probably lead to a greater concentration of wealth. But perhaps most important, income is a better measure of ability to pay than consumption and it would be unwise to depart from this familiar and widely-approved basis of taxation.

Adjustment of Taxes for Inflation

With the continued high rates of inflation, more and more people are being persuaded that the income taxes should be adjusted for inflation. Few forecasters now believe that the U.S. inflation rate will average much less than 7 percent in the decade of the 1980s and some believe that it will be higher. At such rates, the value of the dollar will be cut at least in half by 1990. It is argued that the income tax was never intended to apply to nominal incomes under such inflationary conditions.

Increases in effective tax rates on incomes that reflect real growth seem to be tolerable, but they are much less tolerable when a significant part of income increases reflects inflation. Inflation affects real tax burdens in two ways. First, the real income component of nominal incomes varies widely depending on the composition of incomes and the length of time over which the income was generated. Second, taxpayers' incremental incomes are thrown into higher tax brackets and effective rates increase even when there is no increase in real incomes. If the inflation component were the same for all types of incomes, the effect of inflation would be limited to the bracket effect which could easily be moderated or eliminated by *ad hoc* or automatic adjustments of the tax bracket limits, personal exemptions, and other structural features of the income tax denominated in dollar terms. But the adjustment of the tax base for inflation is another matter. Explicit rules would be needed to enable millions of taxpayers to make the necessary adjustments and these would differ for different types of income.

Tax administrators generally believe that it is impractical to adjust an income tax fully for inflation. In countries where some form of indexation has been adopted, practices vary widely. In the usual case, the tax brackets and personal exemptions are adjusted either partially or fully for changes in prices. Few countries make adjustments to the tax base and, in most cases, the adjustments are confined to selected sources of income.

Economists are generally very unrealistic about the practicability of complete indexation. In the first place, full indexation would require adding to the tax base the gains from inflation, as well as subtracting the losses. All debtors would be required to include in their taxable income the decline in the real value of their debts, while creditors would be allowed a corresponding deduction for the erosion of the real value of their claims. The gainers from inflation include homeowners, households with installment debt, and such heavy corporate borrowers as public utilities, transportation companies, banks, and other financial institutions, while the losers would include individuals who are net lenders on balance and business firms that rely heavily on equity rather than debt capital. I would personally favor making such corrections to income but, with the large amount of debt in the economy, the wholesale shift in tax burdens implied by indexation would probably be politically unacceptable. In particular, history suggests that taxation of homeowners on their true incomes is a figment of the imagination of tax purists (like me).

Second, the problems of adjusting particular sources of income for inflation are enormous. No correction is necessary for earned incomes because they give the recipients command over resources in the prices of the period during which income is earned and taxed. In the case of income from property, the owner does not receive any additional resources to save or to spend unless his income exceeds the rate of inflation. Thus the inflationary component of nominal interest receipts must be removed from the tax base in a real income tax system. Given the widespread use of computers, the necessary adjustments could easily be made for the taxpayer by financial institutions and most corporations. But for the vast amount of interest paid outside the organized financial sector (mainly direct personal and business lending by one individual to another), the calculations would have to be made by the taxpayer and the possibility of error or cheating in such calculations will be large.

Income from business activity is affected by inflation because depreciation and inventory allowances are based on historical costs and no allowance is made for gains and losses on borrowed capital. The law already allows firms to use the last-in, first-out method of inventory accounting, which in effect permits them to charge inventories at close to current cost. However, the use of historical cost for the calculation of depreciation allowances means that business recovers its investment costs in depreciated dollars. To correct for inflation, the depreciation allowance can be adjusted for increases in the general price level or a deduction can be provided currently so that the cost of the investment is recovered in the same prices as when the investment is made. (A method of calculating such an adjustment is discussed below.) Gains and losses on borrowed capital should not be too difficult for business firms to calculate.

If these corrections were made, corporate dividends or equity distributions of noncorporate business would be paid out from inflation-corrected profits, so that no further adjustments would be needed for such income receipts. However, corporations as a group retain a significant proportion of their earnings, and these retentions are presumably reflected in the value of their securities. When securities are sold, the capital gains and losses realized by the owners will reflect the effect of inflation as well as the earnings retained by the corporation, and an adjustment would be required for the former.

An elegant solution for the treatment of capital gains in an inflation-adjusted tax system would be to tax such gains on an accrual basis, so that adjustments for inflation would be made currently as in the case of interest. Unfortunately, it is still impractical to calculate accrued capital gains on nonlisted securities, small enterprises, real estate, and other infrequently traded assets, so that the realization principle must be retained. If gains continue to be taxed only on realization, the Internal Revenue Service would be required to provide tables showing the adjustment to the basis of capital assets to be made in the calculation of capital gains, which would depend on the number of years the assets were held. Such tables would not be complicated or long, at least initially, because the inflation correction would presumably be limited to the changes in prices after enactment of the legislation, but they would become lengthy eventually.

If an inflation correction were made for capital gains, three other adjustments to the tax law would be appropriate. First, the rate of tax on capital gains (now set at 40 percent of the regular rates) ought to be set at the level of regular rates, since the preferential rate is justified in large part on the grounds that nominal capital gains reflect inflation in varying degrees. (Some would argue for continuation of the preferential capital gains rate on incentive grounds, but there is little reason to favor capital gains over other property incomes in a real income tax system, particularly since capital gains are already eligible for five-year averaging under the present system.) Second, capital gains on assets transferred by gift are now subject to tax only when the heirs dispose of the assets and gains transferred at death escape tax completely. Such gains should be regarded as realized when the transfers are made so that a tax would be paid on capital gains at least once in a lifetime. Third, given the use of the realization principle, the interest on the tax that is deferred during the periodassets are held should be included in the tax base at the same time the inflation adjustment is introduced. The value of this deferral is real income and it can be substantial.

The adjustment of the tax brackets and the personal exemptions for inflation presents no particular administrative problem, but the question here is whether the adjustment should be made automatically or on a discretionary basis. Until 1981, Congress adjusted the tax brackets and the exemptions periodically on an *ad hoc* basis; under the 1981 act, these adjustments will be made automatically beginning in 1985. The major argument for automatic adjustment is that the increases in effective rates are unintentional by-products of inflation. On the other hand, automatic adjustment presupposes that the degree of progression in the rate structure when the legislation is enacted is "correct" in some sense. Most supporters of automatic adjustment believe that restraining the growth of revenues would restrain the growth of federal expenditures, but it is not clear that this is necessarily the case.

I conclude that it is impractical to design and implement a tax system that would be applied to real income rather than nominal income. Of the two types of adjustments needed to correct for inflation, adjustment of the tax base is more important than adjustment of the tax brackets and exemptions, but it is impractical to make all the necessary adjustments to the tax base. Under the circumstances, it is best to confine the inflation adjustments to the most essential ones and to avoid favoring some groups over others. Since productivity and growth are related to business investment, I would place highest priority on the adoption of a method to correct depreciation allowances for inflation. Adjustment of property income for inflation should be made only if the preferential capital gains rate is eliminated, capital gains transferred by gift or at death are taxed as if realized, a correction for tax deferral is made, and similar treatment is accorded to recipients of interest and capital gains. It should be obvious that any extensive amount of indexing will require the enactment of tax rate increases by Congress or large cuts in outlays to avoid excessively large deficits in the federal budget. Finally, indexation would reduce the stabilizing effect of the income tax during periods of growth and inflation and might reduce the government's resolve to fight inflation.

The Corporation Income Tax

The corporation income tax has been a basic source of federal revenue since its enactment in 1909, but it has contributed a declining share of total receipts in recent years. It generated 30 percent of federal receipts in fiscal year 1955, 20 percent in 1969, 15 percent in 1974, and an estimated 13 percent in 1980. Although it has demonstrated its survival powers, the corporation income tax is constantly under attack.

The basic problem is that a tax on the net income of corporations does not have the same type of rationale as a tax on the net income of individuals. The major justification for it in principle is that the corporation is a vehicle for accumulating capital which is managed and controlled by the corporate officers and directors and is not subject to the control of the stockholders. This type of economic power, it is believed, is a proper basis for taxation. The major practical justification is that the corporation income tax is needed to safeguard the individual income tax. Without it, individuals could amass huge amounts of wealth in corporations which would never be subject to tax or would be taxed under the current system at preferential rates.

Opponents of the present system argue that, since corporate earnings are taxed at the individual as well as the corporate levels, the corporation tax places a heavy burden on capital and discourages private investment. Since dividends are subject to tax while interest is not, the present system also encourages debt over equity financing.

For these reasons, proposals are continuously being made to "integrate" the corporation and individual income taxes in some fashion. The theoretically "correct" method would be to treat corporations as if they are partnerships and tax shareholders on their shares of the profits, while the corporate tax would be used as a withholding tax. But experts agree that this method is technically impractical because of such problems as basis adjustment for corporate tax withheld at the source, the virtual impossibility of satisfactorily allocating losses among part-year and full-year shareholders, and the treatment of amended returns and audit adjustments for earlier tax years. Furthermore, it would be impractical to ask stockholders to pay full tax on income that they do not actually receive (even though part of the tax was withheld at the source).

As an alternative to full integration, proponents support the adoption of some form of partial integration under which a deduction or credit would be provided under the individual income tax for taxes presumably paid on dividends at the corporate level. Dividend relief would moderate or eliminate the additional tax burden of the corporate tax on earnings paid out by corporations, but the tax on retained earnings would remain. While this type of relief has strong support among tax experts and key legislative figures, it is not without its problems. Perhaps most important, dividend relief would probably be unacceptable unless something were done to avoid giving a deduction or credit for income paid out of corporate earnings on which U.S. tax had not been paid. Such earnings are large relative to total corporate earnings because the law contains numerous provisions which reduce or wipe out the U.S. tax, e.g., the investment credit, the foreign tax credit, deductions for intangible drilling expenses, the exclusion of interest on state and local bonds, and so on. If dividend relief were denied to earnings from such sources, the objectives of the preferences would be thwarted. If distinctions among preferences were made, the mechanics would be hopelessly complicated.

Furthermore, dividend relief proposals will have the effect of encouraging larger dividend payouts by corporations. The retained earnings of corporations are a large source of saving in the United States, and it would seem unwise to encourage any reductions in this source at a time when it is agreed that more saving and investment are needed. Given that the revenues available for tax cutting are small, such a change could hardly be justified under present and foreseeable conditions.

Many business leaders had second thoughts when the full implications of dividend relief were revealed in the debate over this issue in 1977 and 1978. They concluded—in my view, correctly—that, when there is room for cutting taxes on corporate earnings, a reduction in the corporation income tax rates would be simpler than dividend relief and would do less damage to saving and investment.

Priorities for Tax Reform

The foregoing discussion suggests that there are no panaceas in tax policy for the nation's economic ills. Nor is there any reason to make radical changes in the federal tax system in the expectation that they will produce miracles. Notwithstanding its defects, the U.S. federal tax system is probably the best in the world. It produces a large amount of revenue but it is less burdensome than most systems, it is moderately progressive, and compliance is high. (Recent scare stories about the "hidden economy" are sheer exaggerations. The hidden economy is much smaller relative to the size of the economy in the United States than in other countries and there is no evidence that it has been growing faster than the economy as a whole.) The priorities for tax reform should be to make those changes that would clearly promote the nation's economic objectives and improve the equity of the tax system so that it will be more acceptable to the average taxpayer.

I believe that economic objectives in the next several years would best be served if the scarce funds available for tax cuts were used to correct depreciation allowances for inflation and to reduce the payroll tax rate. The depreciation correction would buttress investment, which in the long run will contribute modestly to productivity growth.

The payroll tax cut would reduce business costs and bring down prices somewhat and would also improve tax equity. Looking beyond these changes, the major focus of long-run tax reform should be to improve the individual income tax, which should remain the basic source of federal revenue.

DEPRECIATION REFORM

Between 1971 and 1981, businesses were authorized to depreciate their assets over a 20-percent shorter time period than the officially approved useful lives. This system initially provided more liberalized depreciation than was needed to calculate net income, but inflation seriously eroded the value of the allowances. A proposal to correct this situation that was enacted in modified form by Congress in 1981 was to substitute the three-step 10-5-3 system of depreciation write-offs for the old system. The new system permits firms to depreciate structures over ten to twenty years, equipment over five years, and up to $100,000 of cars and light trucks over three years.

As compared to the old system of depreciation based on asset lives, the new system will greatly distort business investment. It will be a bonanza for those who invest in long-lived assets (such as public utilities, shopping centers, and commercial buildings), while giving little additional tax reduction to those who already depreciate their assets over the shorter periods. Furthermore, the system will generate a huge revenue loss—as much as $60 billion after five years—yet the erosion of depreciation allowances through inflation would not be solved. I would prefer a less radical change in depreciation which would establish neutrality among assets of varying durability and also permanently resolve the inflation problem.

The most innovative idea of adjusting the system of tax depreciation that I have seen to date is to allow an immediate deduction for the present value of the future economic depreciation that firms could claim if there were no inflation. This idea was originally conceived by Nicholas Kaldor and has recently been rediscovered by Alan J. Auerbach and Dale W. Jorgenson. The plan has two virtues: First, all assets would be taxed on their full economic net income (to the extent that the wastage of assets in production can be approximated in practice); and, second, no adjustment for inflation would ever be needed because the depreciation deduction would be taken in the same year in which the asset was purchased. The budget consequences of this change would initially be considerable, so that some phase-in would be needed before such a system can be fully implemented. To achieve neutrality among assets, it would also be necessary to repeal the investment credit. If a neutral stimulus for investment is desired, the stimulus should be provided through an initial allowance which would be deducted from the cost of the asset before the depreciation allowance is calculated.

THE PAYROLL TAX

The payroll tax is the basic source of financing of the social security system. The tax is paid equally by both employers and employees on earnings up to a maximum stipulated in the law. As social security benefits have increased, the tax rates and the amount of earnings subject to tax have increased sharply. The latest schedule of increases was enacted in 1977, when it became clear that additional financing would be needed to keep the social security trust funds financially viable. The January 1, 1981 increases under this legislation amount to $13 billion at an annual rate. On that date, the payroll tax rate for em-

ployers and employees rose from 6.13 to 6.65 percent
and the earnings limit increased from $25,900 to
$29,700(the limit would have moved to $27,800 if
it were adjusted only for inflation).

The use of the payroll tax in social security financing
was originally justified on the ground that social security
was a form of insurance. It is generally agreed that the insurance analogy no longer fits the system very well. All
beneficiaries so far have received far larger benefits than
would be justified by their taxes and accumulated interest,
and many beneficiaries will continue to do so indefinitely.
The system is not funded, so that the payroll taxes are not
stored up or invested but are paid out currently as benefits. In effect, benefits are financed out of taxes paid currently by the working generation.

Since it is used for financing an ongoing federal program,
the payroll tax should be evaluated like any other major
tax of the federal revenue system. On this basis, the payroll tax fares poorly. In the first place, the tax is proportional up to the earnings limit and regressive thereafter. This is in sharp contrast to the individual income
tax, which exempts income deemed essential for a minimum living standard and is graduated above that level.
Second, the tax paid by employers enters into business
costs and thus raises prices. The large increases in payroll
taxes in recent years have undoubtedly contributed
through automatic or negotiated adjustments of wages to
changes in consumer prices. Given the current inflationary
situation, it made no sense to accept a payroll tax increase
that added $6.5 billion to employer costs in 1981.

While it is impractical at this stage to turn the clock back
completely, there are a number of ways to reduce the reli-
ance of the federal tax system on the payroll tax. First,
future increases in payroll tax rates could be replaced by
general revenues. A simple but effective step would be to

rescind the 1981 rate increase and reimburse the trust funds from the general fund. Second, a credit against the individual and corporation income taxes could be provided for some portion of the payroll tax paid. Taxpayers with children are already allowed to credit 10 percent of the first $5,000 of their earnings against their income tax. (The credit is phased out as the adjusted gross income of the taxpayer rises from $6,000 to $10,000 and it is refundable to earners who are not subject to tax.) Eligibility for the credit could be expanded to include taxpayers without children and credit could be provided (at a reduced rate) for earnings above $5,000. Along this line, legislation has been introduced in Congress to provide an income tax credit to employees and employers for the entire 1981 payroll tax increase. It would be better to reduce payroll tax rates directly, but the credit approach has the practical political virtue that the payroll tax revenues remain in the social security trust funds and no general revenue allocation is formally needed.

A third method, proposed by the 1979 Advisory Council on Social Security, would be to shift the payroll tax receipts of the hospital insurance fund to the retirement and disability funds and use general revenues to finance the hospital fund. Benefits under the hospital program for the aged are not related to wages, so that there is no justification for using a payroll tax to finance these benefits. The Advisory Council recommended that part of the payroll tax from the hospital fund should be used to finance retirement and disability benefits over the next 45 years and that the remainder should be eliminated. However, it now appears that all the revenues of the hospital fund will be needed for retirement and disability purposes. The shift proposed by the Advisory Council would at least forestall future increases in payroll taxes. My own preference would be to cut payroll taxes from their present levels and use general revenues to make up the revenue loss.

THE INDIVIDUAL INCOME TAX

Recent legislative experience with the individual income tax is not encouraging. The base-broadening movement made some headway in the 1960s and early 1970s when the minimum tax was adopted, tax shelter loopholes were curtailed, percentage depletion was eliminated for large oil producers, and some unnecessary personal deductions were eliminated. But there has been considerable retrogression in the last several years. New tax credits have been adopted to promote everything from the installment of storm windows and clock thermostats in residences to the creation of jobs for unemployed workers. The gap between the tax rates on capital gains and those on ordinary income has widened and home owners have been given a huge additional preference (exemption of the first $100,000 of capital gains on residences of persons over 55 years of age). As a result, horizontal equity has deteriorated and the tax law and tax returns have become even more complicated. At the same time, only a beginning has been made to resolve the issue of the tax treatment of two-earner married couples, which generates an enormous amount of needless ill will toward the income tax. Congress continues to resist broadening the withholding system to improve compliance and no progress has been made to simplify the tax return for the taxpayers who must use the long form (Form 1040). These problems can be resolved, but only if Congress reverses its current attitude of hostility toward rational income taxation. A minimum agenda includes pruning the list of tax expenditures, resolving the issue of the tax treatment of two-earner married couples, implementing withholding on interest and dividends, and simplifying the tax return.

Tax expenditures. The Budget Act of 1974 directed the president to include in his annual budget a list of tax expenditures. The term is officially defined to mean provisions in the tax law which are exceptions to the "normal" structure of the individual and corporation income taxes. Such items are regarded as "expenditures" to remind us that frequently the tax provisions are really government payments and that the same objectives could be accomplished by direct outlays that are subject to scrutiny in the budget process rather than by income tax exclusions, deductions, or credits which are reviewed only rarely. The total of tax expenditures is now very large: for fiscal year 1982, they will be about a third of direct outlays in the federal budget. In recent years, Congress has greatly expanded the list of tax expenditures, particularly in the category of tax credits for energy-saving outlays by both individuals and businesses. The new tax expenditures enacted since 1975 have added over $25 billion to the total (at 1981 income levels) and the amount continues to rise with the passage of every revenue act. The first requirement of a rational tax policy is to stop further hemorrhaging of the tax base and then to eliminate the least defensible eroding features of the income tax law. The following six areas illustrate the problems.

1) The tax exemption privilege for interest on state and local bonds reduces revenues of federal government much more than it reduces interest costs to state and local governments. In addition, these governments have been issuing tax-exempt revenue bonds to finance such private investments as airport facilities, pollution-control equipment, sports arenas, convention halls, and nonprofit hospitals. The distortion of the intent of the tax exemption has become more blatant as the states have recently begun issuing revenue bonds to finance student loans and middle- and high-income housing backed by federal loans and guarantees. The amounts involved now run into the tens of billions of dollars. Congress has been trying for several years to limit this practice to bonds that finance low-cost housing,

but even this mild provision has not yet been approved. Assuming some federal assistance for state-local borrowing is desirable, the appropriate action would be to limit the federal subsidy to general obligations of the state and local governments, and to convert the subsidy from a tax exemption to a payment for part of the interest due on eligible securities. This could be done by allowing individuals and corporations to deduct the subsidy as a credit against their income taxes. A tax credit of 35–40 percent of the interest would *increase* the effective subsidy to state and local governments and save money for the federal government.

2) Before 1976, the capital gain on property transferred at death was completely exempt. Congress then enacted a provision requiring recipients of bequests to pay tax on this gain when they sold the asset. However, Congress delayed implementation of the provision until 1980 and, in the interim, opponents of the provision succeeded in getting it repealed altogether. The original provision was not optimum in any event because it would have locked up assets in portfolios of wealthy people for years, if not generations. The appropriate treatment is to tax the gains on all assets transferred either at gift or death. At present, individuals who must sell assets during life for business or other reasons pay tax on their gains, while those who are able to hold on to their assets until death are exempt. The lock-in effect reduces the mobility of capital and the income that escapes taxation is large.

3) In 1980, Congress increased the $100 dividend exclusion to $200 ($400 on joint returns) and expanded the exclusion to include interest. The provision originally applied to the years 1981 and 1982, at a cost of $2 billion a year, but was then limited to one year. It was allegedly designed to increase saving, but the effect was negligible. About 75 percent of the tax benefit went to taxpayers who already receive $200 of interest and dividends. For these

people, the extra tax benefit is equivalent to a lump-sum tax reduction and had no effect on savings. This is an example of an entirely wasteful tax expenditure and it should be allowed to expire on schedule at the end of 1981.

4) The deductibility of interest payments on borrowed money, accelerated depreciation, and other capital consumption allowances permits investors in highly leveraged assets to "shelter" from tax incomes from other sources for a number of years. These tax shelter arrangements were circumscribed to a degree in 1976 by the requirement that the accounting losses from an investment cannot exceed the amount of capital at risk. However, the provision does not apply to real-estate investments; and, in any event, taxpayers receive the benefits of the large immediate deductions to the extent that they risk their own money. One solution would be to limit the deductions for any particular venture to the gross receipts from that venture (with carry-over of unused deductions to future receipts). In this way, taxpayers would not be allowed to generate artificial tax losses that are now used to shelter incomes from other sources.

5) The tax provisions for the elderly are complicated and give the largest benefits to those with the highest income. The preferences include the extra exemption for the aged, the retirement income credit, and the exclusion of social security benefits from taxable income. The Advisory Commission on Social Security recommended that half of social security benefits be subject to tax, which would mean that an aged couple would not begin to pay any additional tax until its total income exceeded $7,400 and, if its only income were exclusively from social security, it would not pay any tax until benefits exceeded $14,800. Even this compromise would undertax the elderly because the payroll tax contributions plus accumulated interest will account for no more than about 17 percent of the retirement

benefits of current workers. If all the income tax preferences for the aged were removed, the additional revenues could be used to raise retirement and disability benefits or allocated to the trust funds to improve the financial soundness of the social security system.

6) The personal deductions for such outlays as state and local taxes, interest, contributions, and medical expenses are costly and their complexity bedevils both taxpayers and administrators. Moreover, most of these are hard to justify on the basis of tax theory. At a minimum, "floors" should be placed under the deductions for state and local taxes and charitable contributions (as in the case of medical expenses) to limit the deduction to unusual outlays. In the case of interest paid on mortgage and consumer loans, the deduction should be limited to the amount of positive property income reported by taxpayers on their returns (with carry-overs of unused interest deductions to future years) so that they would be allowed to deduct interest when the loans are associated with the production of income, but would not be able to deduct interest on loans that do not produce income. The revenue from such changes would be substantial, and the switch from itemizing deductions to the use of the standard deduction (now incorporated in the first rate bracket which has a zero tax rate) would ease compliance for large numbers of taxpayers.

The family unit. The proper treatment of the two-earner married couple is basically a question of the unit to be used for income taxation. Before 1948, the individual was the basic tax unit and married couples were taxed as separate individuals. In 1930, the Supreme Court ruled that community property laws in eight states were valid for federal income tax purposes, which meant that married couples in community property states could split their income in computing their tax liabilities. Immediately after World War II, a number of other states enacted community property laws for the sole purpose of obtaining the advantages of income splitting for their residents. In addition, married couples in noncommunity property states began splitting their incomes through such devices as family partnerships and gifts. To avoid the disruption of property arrangements and to restore tax equality among married couples, Congress in 1948 extended the privilege of income splitting for tax purposes to all married couples filing joint returns.

The income splitting device achieved geographic tax equality for married couples in a spectacularly successful way. The states that had joined the community property bandwagon for tax reasons alone repealed their community property laws almost immediately. The problems created by family partnerships and gifts became less acute and are rarely mentioned today. Most important, the vast majority of married couples file joint returns and are spared the chore of dividing their incomes, exemptions, and deductions on separate returns.

Unfortunately, these advantages were purchased at a heavy cost in terms of tax equity and, as it turned out, in further complicating the tax law. Since income splitting is confined to married couples, those who are not married cannot receive any benefit from the provision, even though they may have similar family responsibilities. Congress soon learned that it made no sense to draw a sharp dividing line on the basis of marital status alone and began to move the tax burden of single persons closer to that of married couples. Today, widows and widowers are permitted to use the same tax schedule as married couples for two years after the death of a spouse; half the advantage of a joint return is given to single persons who maintain a household for children or other dependents; single persons are given a standard deduction (now the zero rate bracket) of 68 percent of the standard deduction of married couples filing joint returns instead of half; and single persons who are not heads of households are taxed at rates that do not exceed by more than 30 percent the rates of married couples filing joint returns (under pure income splitting, the difference would be as high as 60 percent). As a result of these modifications, taxpayers are now required to choose from among four different sets of tax rates in figuring their tax liabilities. More importantly, some couples pay higher taxes after they are married than they paid before marriage; conversely, other couples pay substantially lower taxes after marriage. A tax law that contains both marital penalties and marital subsidies is considered bizarre by most people, and so it is.

I do not believe it will ever be possible to arrive at a satisfactory solution to these problems merely by adjusting the tax rates. The proper solution is to keep the device of income splitting for married couples (so that geographic equality is maintained), but to tax single persons and married couples filing joint returns at the same rates. (Formally, this is equivalent to retaining income splitting and halving the brackets for married couples, but married couples filing joint returns need not know the difference because they would use the same rate schedule as single persons.) If the present exemptions and deductions do not allow sufficiently for differences in family size, the proper remedy is to change the exemptions or deductions, not to keep juggling the tax rates.

The drawback of taxing all married couples at the same rates is that two-earner married couples pay the same taxes as one-earner married couples with the same income. When income splitting was adopted in 1948, this was not much of a problem because it was considered normal for the husband to work and the wife to remain at home. Today, the majority of married couples have two earners and it is no longer appropriate to treat the one-earner couple as the norm.

To arrive at the appropriate solution, it is necessary to understand what the problem is. Equal treatment of couples with equal total incomes gives the wrong result because married couples with one earner have more taxpaying ability than married couples with two earners. The spouse who does not work produces valuable services that the two-earner couple must buy, but these services cannot be evaluated in money terms and therefore cannot be taxed. Thus it is unfair to tax the combined earnings of the two spouses in full because some part of the earnings is absorbed in meeting these extra expenses.

Many well-meaning people who wish to change the present situation propose that two-earner married couples be permitted to file separate returns. Some confine the separate returns to earnings only, while others would return to the pre-1948 arrangements under which married couples filed separate returns for all the income "owned" by each spouse. While this solution has great appeal to many people, it would make the present mess even worse. First, it would reinstate the old community property problem unless Congress explicitly overruled the splitting of earnings between spouses in community property states, and previous history suggests that this would be difficult. Second, it would restore the advantage of splitting property between spouses in noncommunity property states by various subterfuges. This could be avoided if separate filing were allowed only for earnings, but then some arbitrary method would be required to allocate property income among the spouses. Third, it would be necessary to devise an arbitrary method of allocating deductions between spouses. Simply permitting the deduction to the spouse who writes the check is not satisfactory because many outlays that are deductible under the income tax are made for the benefit of both spouses. Defenders of separate returns for married couples are aware of these problems, but accept them as necessary evils in resolving an issue which they regard as crucial in the fight to obtain equal treatment for women.

I sympathize with those who would reintroduce separate returns, but I strongly believe that theirs would be the wrong approach. The cost of separate returns in tax complexity, litigation, and taxpayer resentment would be enormous. It would be much better to retain the basic principle of joint return filing for married couples but to make a special allowance for the lower taxpaying ability of two-earner couples.

It is obviously impossible to calculate the exact amount by which the taxable income of the one-earner couple is understated as compared with that of the two-earner couple. As a substitute, two-earner couples should be given a flat percentage deduction of the earned income of the spouse with the lower earnings. Congress enacted a 10 percent deduction in 1981 with a limit of $3,000, but I believe the deduction should be more generous—say, 20 percent—and it should be given without limit because the marital penalty extends to the top of the income scale.

In brief, it is possible to retain the present administrative and compliance advantages of income splitting and also to correct the "tax on marriage" that is imposed on two earners. The important ingredients are: first, to keep the mechanics of income splitting for married couples but to equalize the tax rates for married couples and single persons with the same taxable income; second, to reexamine the exemptions and deductions to see whether they differentiate properly among families of different sizes? third, to provide a special deduction for married couples with two earners; fourth, to revise the rates to avoid any significant revenue losses. These changes would shift tax burdens from single persons and married couples with two earners to married couples with one earner. In may opinion, such a shift in relative tax burdens is long overdue on equity and economic grounds.

Withholding on interest and dividends. Present law calls for individuals to report interest and dividends on their tax returns, and the Internal Revenue Service depends on its regular enforcement procedures to detect underreporting. Payers of interest and dividends are required to file information returns for each person receiving $10 or more of such income during the year, but the Internal Revenue Service has never had the resources needed to match the tens of millions of information forms with tax returns. The result has been that compliance in reporting interest and dividends has been poor—particularly interest reporting—and the government is losing more than $3 billion a year of tax revenue.

When the federal income tax was enacted in 1913, withholding was required from interest, rents, wages and salaries, annuities, and incomes other than dividends above $3,000 (dividends were excluded because they were subject to surtax, but not to the normal tax), but the withholding system was abolished in 1917. When it was reintroduced in 1941, withholding was applied only to wages and salaries. The possibility of extending withholding to interest and dividends has been explored frequently since then. The Congress has considered such a provision on several occasions (the House actually passed one in 1942, 1950, 1951, and 1962), but each time the opposition prevailed. In March 1980, the president recommended the adoption of interest and dividend withholding, but Congress virtually ignored the recommendation.

At one time, the excuses for rejecting interest and dividend withholding were that the costs of compliance and administration would be heavy and that tax would be unnecessarily withheld from the receipts of many nontaxable individuals and tax-exempt organizations. Now that information returns are required for annual interest and dividend payments of $10 or more, the marginal costs of compliance and administration would not be large. To keep overwithholding to a minimum, most interest and dividend withholding plans in recent years would have permitted nontaxable individuals and tax-exempt organizations to file exemption certificates with the financial institutions and business firms paying interest and dividends. It is also possible to permit nontaxable interest and dividend recipients to file for refunds of withheld taxes on a quarterly basis if exemption certificates are not sufficient.

The real reason why interest and dividend withholding has been rejected is that banks and saving-and-loan institutions have bitterly opposed it. Their opposition is understandable, since the amount withheld would come out of the earnings normally added to their deposits. The Treasury has on occasion offered to keep the amounts withheld on deposit with these institutions, but this offer has never assuaged the opposition.

Some people have opposed withholding on the ground that it would reduce saving. This argument implies that savers will be discouraged from saving merely because they are required to pay the taxes they owe. Even if there is a small effect on saving, this can hardly be used to justify inaction to improve enforcement of the tax law. If tax rates are too high, they should be reduced for everybody, not just for those who are careless or dishonest.

Income tax simplification. Congress and every administration in recent years have paid lip service to the objective of simplification, but the income tax becomes more and more complicated with the passage of every revenue act. The 1980 income tax return (Form 1040) contained, in addition to a two-page initial summary, 10 separate schedules and 31 supplementary forms for detailed reporting of income receipts, deductions, and credits and for the computation of tax liability. The 1980 form listed seven different adjustments that were allowed in arriving at adjusted gross income and eight different tax credits. In 1960, there was only one adjustment to calculate adjusted gross income and one tax credit. There is no question that income tax reporting has become both aggravating and costly. Public opinion polls invariably report that millions of taxpayers feel that they cannot cope with income tax reporting and must pay for assistance in the preparation of their returns.

The source of the complexity is the attempt by Congress and most administrations to do too much with the income tax. Whether it is promotion of jobs, energy saving, or incentives to work, save and invest, the normal reaction is to add a special deduction or credit to the income tax to help achieve the urgent social objective. Every such departure from the normal structure of the income tax leaves its mark on the tax return and imposes additional burdens of record-keeping for the taxpayer.

The obvious solution is to repeal all the special provisions and start all over again. Chairman Wilbur D. Mills of the Ways and Means Committee introduced a bill along these lines in 1972, but nothing came of it. In fact, he intended the bill to demonstrate that, while simplification is approved by all groups in principle, in practice the forces arrayed against simplification through the elimination of tax preferences are much too powerful to permit any progress to be made in this way.

A second-best solution would be to introduce a simplified income tax as an option for taxpayers to use if it is to their advantage. The simplified tax would include all incomes without any exclusions and would have no personal deductions or tax credits; in effect, the exclusions, deductions, and credits would be reflected in the rate schedule rather than in separate adjustments to arrive at taxable income. Taxpayers would simply add up their income sources, subtract their personal exemptions, and calculate their tax liability from a tax table or the schedule of tax rates. To make the optional tax attractive, the rate schedule would have to be significantly lower than the present one (and the temptation to enact exceptions under the optional tax would have to be resisted). Some experimentation would be needed to see how many taxpayers would find it advantageous to use the simplified tax schedule, but I believe that it would be possible to attract as many as 95 percent of persons filing returns with a rate schedule ranging from 8 percent to 40 percent or even lower. The gain in taxpayer morale and the reduced costs of compliance and administration would be enormous.

Conclusions

The present federal tax system leaves much to be desired, but it is not so defective that it should be assigned to the scrap heap. The tax rates are not punitive, and the degree of progression is relatively mild. The tax system has not caused the slowdown in productivity growth currently being experienced in the United States, and tax reduction will not significantly revive incentives and productivity growth. For this reason, it would be irresponsible to risk large deficits from tax cuts that are not accompanied by corresponding expenditure cuts. The deficits will exacerbate inflation and force the authorities to take restrictive monetary actions to slow down the economy and further reduce investment and growth.

It is unnecessary and unwise to replace part or all of the federal income tax with a consumption tax. The value-added tax is similar to a retail sales tax in almost every respect: it would raise prices by the amount of the tax and it would be regressive. The graduated expenditure tax is more defensible in theory, but the change in the tax base from income to consumption would have unacceptable distributional effects (heavier tax burdens on young and older families and lighter burdens on middle-aged families) and would be difficult to implement.

Indexation of the income tax for inflation is also attractive in theory but difficult in practice. To do a complete job, the tax base as well as the tax brackets and exemptions must be adjusted for inflation. Full adjustment of the tax base would greatly complicate compliance and administration. Whether the tax brackets and exemptions should be adjusted for inflation automatically each year (as Congress now prefers) or on a discretionary basis is a matter of political judgment.

The corporation income tax is an important supplement to the individual income tax. Proposals to integrate the corporation and individual income taxes are impractical, while dividend relief would require distinctions to be made between dividends paid out of taxed and nontaxed corporate earnings. Such distinctions would be resisted by those who benefit from tax preferences and would be complicated. Furthermore, dividend relief would reduce corporate saving. It would be better to retain the corporation tax in its present form and use whatever revenues are available to cut the corporate tax rate.

The most urgent tax changes in current circumstances are to adjust depreciation allowances for inflation and to reduce payroll tax rates. Depreciation reform would help sustain investment and promote productivity growth. The payroll tax cut would improve tax equity, reduce business costs, and lower the price level.

In the long run, an effort should be made to improve the individual income tax. This is the best and most productive tax in the revenue system and we should do everything we can to broaden the tax base in order to bring the tax rates down. The primary objective should be to improve horizontal equity and to simplify the tax so that the ordinary taxpayer will be able to fill out his own tax return and business will be able to conduct its affairs without worrying about the tax implications. The goal should be to reduce the individual income tax rates from the scheduled range of 11–50 percent in 1984 to 8–40 percent or lower.

Bibliographical Notes

Most of the issues discussed in this chapter are covered in Richard A. Musgrave and Peggy Musgrave, *Public Finance in Theory and Practice*, 3rd ed. (New York: McGraw-Hill, 1980). A nontechnical explanation of the issues in individual and corporate income taxation may be found in Joseph A. Pechman's *Federal Tax Policy* 3rd ed. (Washington, D.C.: Brookings Institution, 1977), Chs. 4 and 5.

The literature on the incentive effects of taxation is relatively recent, but it is becoming voluminous. A good summary of the early literature is given by George Break, "The Incidence and Economics Effects of Taxation," in Alan S. Blinder *et al.*, *The Economics of Public Finance* (Washington, D.C.: Brookings Institution, 1974), pp. 119–240. A summary of the most recent empirical work on the effects of taxation on labor supply, saving, private business investment, the stock market, and other economic activities and new estimates of the effects in each area are given in Henry J. Aaron and Joseph A. Pechman, eds., *How Taxes Affect Economic Behavior* (Washington, D.C.: Brookings Institution, 1981).

Summaries of empirical work done on the effects of taxes on labor supply are provided in Institute for Fiscal Studies, *Taxation and Incentives* (London: IFS, 1970); Organization of Economic Co-operation and Development, *Theoretical and Empirical Aspects of the Effects of Taxation on the Supply of Labor* (Paris: OECD, 1975); and Harvey S. Rosen, "What is Labor Supply and Do Taxes Affect It," *American Economic Review*, Vol. 70, May 1980, pp. 171–76. The most recent estimates of the response of labor supply to changes in after-tax earnings are by Jerry A. Hausman, "Labor Supply," in *How Taxes Affect Economic Behavior*.

An early estimate of the response of saving to changes in the rate of interest was made by Colin Wright in "Saving and the Rate of Interest," *The Taxation of Income from Capital*, Arnold C. Harberger and Martin J. Bailey, eds. (Washington, D.C.: Brookings Institution, 1969), p. 275. The highest estimate of the response was made by Michael J. Boskin, "Taxation, Saving and the Rate of Interest," *Journal of Political Economy*, Vol. 86, April 1978, pp. S3–S27. A low response was found by E. Philip Howrey and Saul H. Hymans in "The Measurement and Determination of Loanable-Funds Saving," *Brookings Papers on Economic Activity*, 3:1978, pp. 665–706 and reprinted in Joseph A. Pechman, ed., *What Should be Taxed: Income or Expenditure?* (Washington, D.C.: Brookings Institution, 1979), pp. 1–48. Charles L. McLure, Jr. summarizes the theoretical and empirical controversy on the response of saving to the interest rate in *Taxes, Saving and Welfare: Theory and Evidence*, National Bureau of Economic Research, Working Paper No. 504, July 1980.

Early estimates of the effects of taxation on private business investment are summarized in Gary Fromm, ed., *Tax Incentives and Capital Spending* (Washington, D.C.: Brookings Institution, 1971). For a survey of the literature on the factors influencing investment behavior, see Dale W. Jorgenson, "Econometric Studies of Investment Behavior: A Survey," *Journal of Economic Literature*, Vol. 9, December 1971, pp. 1111–47. A more recent summary of the estimates and a new econometric analysis of the data are provided by Patric H. Hendershott and Sheng-Cheng Hu, "Investment in Producers Equipment," in *How Taxes Affect Economic Behavior*.

For the factors affecting the stock market, see Franco Modigliani and Robert Cohn, "Inflation, Rational Valuation, and the Market," *Financial Analysts Journal*, Vol. 25, No. 2, March–April 1979, pp. 22–24; and Roger Brinner and Stephen Brooks, "Stock Prices," in *How Taxes Affect Economic Behavior*. The response of capital gains realizations to changes in the capital gains tax rate has been estimated by Martin Feldstein, Joel Slemrod, and Shlomo Vitzhaki in "The Effects of Taxation on the Selling of Corporate Stock and the Realization of Capital Gains," *Quarterly Journal of Economics*, Vol. XCIV, June 1980, pp. 777–91; and Joseph J. Minarik, "Capital Gains," in *How Taxes Affect Economic Behavior*.

The relative merits of income and consumption taxes are examined in detail in *The Role of Direct and Indirect Taxes in the Federal Revenue System* (Princeton: Princeton University Press for the National Bureau of Economic Research, 1964); and Richard A. Musgrave, ed., *Broad Based Taxes: New Options and Sources* (Baltimore, Md.: Johns Hopkins University Press, 1973).

The structure of the value-added tax is described in Dan Throop Smith, James B. Webber, and Carol M. Cerf, *What You Should Know About the Value Added Tax* (Dow Jones–Irwin, 1973). The merits of the value-added tax and other taxes are discussed by the Advisory Commission on Intergovernmental Relations in *The Value-Added Tax and Alternative Sources of Revenue* (Washington, D.C.: Government Printing Office, 1973); and Charles E. McLure and Norman B.

Ture, "Value-Added Tax: Two Views," *Perspectives on Tax Reform* (American Enterprise Institute, 1974).

John Stuart Mill's ideas about the graduated expenditure tax are given in his *Principles of Political Economy*, 5th ed. (Appleton and Company, 1974), vol. 2, pp. 415–29. Irving Fisher's ideas are presented in his *Constructive Income Taxation* (New York: Harper, 1941). The classic book on the expenditure tax is Nicholas Kaldor's *An Expenditure Tax* (London: Allen and Unwin, 1955). A model of the design of an expenditure tax is given in U.S. Department of the Treasury, *Blueprints for Basic Tax Reform* (Washington, D.C.: Government Printing Office, 1977), Chs. 4 and 6. The merits of the income tax and the expenditure tax are compared in Joseph A. Pechman, ed., *What Should Be Taxed: Income or Expenditure?* (Washington, D.C.: Brookings Institution, 1979).

The basic book on inflation accounting for tax purposes is Henry J. Aaron, ed., *Inflation and the Income Tax* (Washington, D.C.: Brookings Institution, 1976). A specific set of indexing revisions is proposed by William Fellner, Kenneth W. Clarkson, and John H. Moore, in *Correcting Taxes for Inflation* (American Enterprise Institute, 1975). Estimates of business profits adjusted for inflation are given by John B. Shoven and Jeremy I. Bulow, "Inflation Accounting and Nonfinancial Corporate Profits: Financial Assets and Liabilities," *Brookings Papers on Economic Activity*, 1:1976, pp. 15–57.

Richard Goode's *The Corporation Income Tax* (New York: Wiley, 1951) provides a thorough analysis and appraisal of the role of the corporation income tax. The economic effects of the corporation income tax are analyzed by Mervyn King, in *Public Policy and the Corporation* (London: Chapman and Hall, 1977); and J. Gregory Ballentine, *Equity, Efficiency and the U.S. Corporation Income Tax* (American Enterprise Institute, 1980). For a strong defense of the idea of integrating the corporation and individual income taxes, see Charles E. McClure, Jr., "Integration of the Personal and Corporate Income Taxes: The Missing Element in Recent Tax Reform Proposals," *Harvard Law Review*, vol. 88, January 1975, pp. 532–82. The practical problems of integration are discussed in detail by Charles E. McClure in *Must Corporate Income Be Taxed Twice?* (Washington, D.C.: Brookings Institution, 1979).

The proposal to provide a deduction for the discounted value of economic depreciation in the year an investment is made is explained in Alan J. Auerbach and Dale W. Jorgenson, *The First Year Capital Recovery System*, Harvard Institute of Economic Research, Discussion Paper Number 740, February 1980. The 10–5–3 depreciation proposal is analyzed in a pamphlet by the American Enterprise Institute, *The Capital Cost Recovery Act Proposal* (American Enterprise Institute, 1980).

The history, rationale and economic effects of the payroll tax are discussed in Joseph A. Pechman's *Federal Tax Policy*, Ch. 7. The proposals of the 1979 Advisory Council on Social Security are presented in its report *Social Security Financing and Benefits* (Washington, D.C.: Government Printing Office, 1980).

The tax expenditure budget is presented in the president's annual budget. The most recent list of tax expenditures is given in *Special Analyses, Budget of the United States Government, Fiscal Year 1981* (Washington, D.C.: Government Printing Office, 1980), pp. 202-38. Stanley S. Surrey, who introduced the concept in policy discussions, describes the rationale of tax expenditures and outlines methods of reforming the tax system in *Pathways of Tax Reform, The Concept of Tax Expenditures* (Cambridge, Mass.: Harvard University Press, 1973).

The operation of tax shelters is explained in a report by the Joint Committee on Taxation, *Overview of Tax Shelters* (Washington, D.C.: Government Printing Office, 1975), and Surrey, *Pathways to Tax Reform*.

The problems of defining the appropriate family unit for income taxation and proposals for revising the present system are explained in Joseph A. Pechman, *Federal Tax Policy*, pp. 92-97. The pros and cons of recent proposals to eliminate the marriage tax penalty are discussed in Joint Committee on Taxation, *The Income Tax Treatment of Married Couples and Single Persons* (Washington, D.C.: Government Printing Office, 1980).

An analysis of the considerations for and against withholding on interest and dividends and an explanation how such withholding could operate are given in Joseph A. Pechman, "Withholding on Interest and Dividends," *Tax Revision Compendium*, Committee on Ways and Means, Vol. 3 (Washington, D.C.: Government Printing Office, 1959). pp. 1479-98. For a description of various proposals, see Joint Taxation Committee, *Description of Proposals Relating to Interest and Dividends* (Washington, D.C.: Government Printing Office, 1980).

Methods of simplifying the individual income tax are analyzed in Joint Taxation Committee, *Issues in Simplification of the Income Tax Laws* (Washington, D.C.: Government Printing Office, 1977) and Charles H. Gustafson, ed., *Federal Income Tax Simplification* (American Law Institute and American Bar Association, 1979). Congressman Wilbur D. Mills' proposal to terminate all special provisions in the tax law is described in Committee on Ways and Means, *Material Relating to H. R. 15230, The Proposed Tax Policy Review Act of 1972* (Washington, D.C.: Government Printing Office, 1972).

Richard A. Musgrave: Comment

We have heard various people testify to the hardships which they endured under Walter's merciless if joyful working habits during the Kennedy council. Let me add a counterexample, giving a fine case of complementarity in utility functions. Back in 1951, Walter and I, together with Alvin Hansen, undertook an AID mission to Bad Godesberg, designed to show that the German economy possessed a greater degree of recuperative power than Bonn expected at that time. In the process, we arrived at a working schedule whereby Walter would start late in the day, work into the early hours of the morning, and then leave his papers under my door. I would be ready to receive them and to pass my contribution to him at lunch. We would take off the afternoon, swimming down the Rhine with Alvin trotting beside and carrying our towels. This, in more important ways, he did for all of us on many occasions. As the intellectual godfather of Bob's "nostra," how delighted would he have been to join in this homage to Walter!

Turning to my assignment, you will not be surprised to find agreement with most of Joe Pechman's fine paper. This is to be expected, since we share the basic principles to which a good tax structure should conform. Equity, and horizontal equity in particular, is an essential ingredient. Other objectives cannot be excluded from the policy, but they should be pursued with minimum damage to equity and only if there are no other and better ways. We agree also that the specifics of tax policy cannot be resolved without reference to an overall norm of good tax structure. The vision of a broad and uniform tax base, combined with lower rates, is one of these norms which he has championed over the years. As noted yesterday, he shared the night vigils of the Heller council, and tax reform was part of its message. My role as discussant, however, is not to praise the Pechman doctrine, especially since much of it is also mine. Rather, it is to raise some questions and perhaps make some additions.

I begin with the response of the income tax to inflation. Joe, of course, recognizes that equity considerations must relate to real rather than to nominal income and he notes that a tax law which is based almost entirely on nominal values is distorted by inflation. But he hesitates to do much about it except for revising depreciation. As I see it, more comprehensive measures are needed. Failure to face up to the problem has been a major, if not the major, factor in the growing disrepute of the income tax. As Joe points out, complete inflation-proofing is impossible, but so is perfection in any task of tax reform. Indexing of rate brackets and exemptions is long overdue. While Congress has offset a substantial part of the revenue gain from bracket creep by *ad hoc* changes in the law, these changes have produced a substantial rearrangement of the tax burden. From 1970 to 1978, a taxpayer with half the median income experienced a reduction in effective rate of about one-third, while the median taxpayer had an increase of about one-quarter. This shift may have been desirable, but it occurred in a hidden and surreptitious fashion which has added greatly to taxpayer dissatisfaction. Nor do I have much sympathy with permitting Congress to enjoy the glory of tax reductions which, in fact, are only offsets to automatic increases in rates. Tax changes ought to be open and aboveboard and not be brought about in a hidden fashion through inflation. Indexing may weaken the anti-inflationary corrective of built-in revenue growth, but I am willing to pay this price. Moreover, actual fiscal behavior (contrary to the textbook premise) may well cause rising revenue to induce rising outlay.

In addition to bracket indexing, capital gains should be adjusted for inflation, and I agree with Joe that this should be combined with taxation at full rates and constructive realization at death. There should also be an adjustment for inflation in the creditor–debtor position. With a real rate of interest which is negative, especially for modest savers, it is hardly appropriate to tax such nominal returns. As to depreciation, I prefer outright indexing of the base to the Kaldor–Jorgenson–Auerbach scheme, but they are essentially similar and either will do. As Joe points out, both are preferable to an arbitrary shortening of asset lives which does not really take care of the inflation problem. In principle, the depreciation adjustment should be combined with corrections for changes in the real value of indebtedness, but in practice it may be necessary to accept the former only.

I would not lay so much stress on inflation adjustment were it not for the dismal prospect of continuing severe inflation. I see no way of resolving the inflation problem without a temporary freeze, followed by a period of active incomes policy and sustained by appropriate demand management. But this remedy is rejected by most of the profession, including our group here. TIP type measures may be of some help, but they require the same apparatus as a more direct approach. Moreover, I greatly fear that they would prove the ultimate tax expenditure which breaks the camel's (income tax) back. I must, therefore, adjust my thinking to the prospect of continuing inflation. The income tax should be inflation-proofed, and it should not be saddled with a TIP burden. If a carrot rather than stick approach to persuasion is wanted, let it be on the expenditure side of the budget.

Apart from inflation, there remain the traditional problems of loophole closing. But loophole closing thrives better (though far from well) in an atmosphere of rising rather than falling revenue needs. Meeting additional revenue needs by plugging loopholes is hard enough, but lowering taxes around loopholes (as hydraulic engineers well know) is beyond hope. Joe is sympathetic to the idea of offering a tax option which would apply a lower set of rates to gross income, but this may be dumping the baby with the bathwater. I would rather stand still (apart from inflation adjustments) and wait for a better time. (Walter's return?) In fact, we may well have gone too far in talking down the income tax. Carter's statement, early in his first campaign, that the income tax is a disgrace, was just that. The income tax, even as is, is a lot better than many of the alternatives, such as the value-added tax.

The idea of a personal and progressive expenditure tax (viewed, as I like to, from the angle of horizontal equity) could be a different matter. The present (at birth) value of potential consumption may well be a better index of "equal position" than is income. Given some very strong and unrealistic assumptions (e.g., perfect credit markets, certainty, no changes in tax rates, etc.), lifetime consumption (plus, I would insist, gifts and bequests) may make for a better base. But these assumptions are farfetched, and Joe is surely correct in warning against comparing a perfect consumption with an imperfect income tax. To be sure, the expenditure tax does not have to deal with the problems of changing asset values which so bug the income tax, and this is its great advantage under inflation. On the other hand, Joe is right in expecting that, given their time, tax lawyers would come up with expenditure-tax loopholes which can as yet not be foreseen. I would not mind replacing some part of the income tax with an honest-to-goodness expenditure tax, but I am strongly opposed to using the expenditure-tax argument as a way of weakening the income tax; and this, in practice, may well be what the game is all about.

Before moving on, let me reflect for a moment on how the new school of "optimal taxation" fits into the thinking of Joe's and my (and also Walter's) generation of tax economists. Which is better, the "good" tax structure of the Simons tradition or the "optimal" one which now emerges? According to Webster, of course, optimal beats good, but the issue is too important to be settled by semantics. Whereas our emphasis has been on horizontal equity, that of the new school is on efficiency. There is merit on both sides. We have been guilty of insufficient attention to dead weight losses, but the new model falls short by disregarding horizontal equity. The essential equity problem is ruled out by considering a setting where all taxpayers have the same utility functions, so that the problem becomes one of minimizing the burden on a single taxpayer. To reconcile the two approaches, tax burden should indeed be defined to include dead weight loss. But having done so, the burden should be distributed among people with different tastes so as to 1) assign equal burdens to people in equal position, and 2) minimize efficiency loss. Where the two objectives differ, an explicit tradeoff is required. Formulating the problem thusly complicates matters, but unless we do we remain well inside the optimality frontier.

There remains taxation under supply-side economics. How can the tax system be used to raise capacity output as distinct from its role in affecting aggregate demand? To begin with, note that this is not the same as minimizing dead weight loss: to induce people to work more by giving a subsidy is no less distorting than to reduce effort by applying a tax. The same holds for investment. However, let me accept the premise that output *is* to be increased. Obviously, the remedy must depend on the disease. To begin with, the problem may be due to insufficient capital formation. As Joe noted, the ratio of plant and equipment expenditure has stood up but the capital to labor ratio has fallen, and additional capital formation is needed to adapt to rising energy costs and environmental protection. In this context, is our concern with inadequate saving or lacking investment incentives? If the shortfall is in saving, is the need for internal funds or outside capital? If the lack is in willingness to invest, are we concerned with total investment or with the investment mix? Alternatively, the problem may be due to inadequate R and D, ineffective education, lacking work incentives, poor managerial quality, and a set of other reasons which have been noted in yesterday's discussion. These questions need to be answered to some extent at least, if the appropriate tax responses are to be devised. Otherwise, we are in the position of a doctor who is to prescribe after being told only that the patient is not well. Nor can we solve the problem by doing everything that may help. Dispensing tax medicine is not free but costly—costly, I mean, not only in revenue which can be made up but also because of its implications for tax equity.

There are some moves which would be helpful on both equity and incentive grounds. Most important among these would be discontinuation of the preferential treatment of owner-occupied housing, a factor which has surely helped to divert capital from productivity-increasing uses to consumption. Another change which would be helpful on both grounds and, I feel, not quite as difficult to apply as Joe believes, would be to integrate the corporate with the personal income tax. Simply cutting corporate tax rates won't do because it strengthens the use of the corporation as a tax haven. In most instances, however, investment incentives hurt equity as they result in unequal treatment of various income sources. Moreover, one need not be unduly cynical to note that tax changes to aid investment also tend to be changes that will aid high-income recipients. Such is the case simply because investment decisions are made mostly by people in the higher brackets. This makes it difficult to distinguish bona fide advocacy of growth from intentions to redistribute the tax burden. It is important, therefore, to find ways which tend to neutralize the distributional implications of growth-oriented changes in the tax structure. For instance, I would prefer to have the dividend-interest exclusion vanish as such income rises, rather than to remove it as Joe suggests. But this is only a small point. Much more attention need be given to deal with the broader issue of developing growth measures which are distributionally neutral or even helpful. Employment as well as investment credits should be considered. The investment credit or, perhaps, an initial allowance, should be rendered as potent as possible. Not all investment incentives are equally good. A marginal credit, for instance, will have a much higher benefit-cost ratio (measured as magnitude of investment effect relative to loss of tax equity) than does further untaxing of capital gains. The tax system should contribute to growth policy, but it should do so as effectively as possible.

A final issue—and here Joe and I may disagree—is the future of social security finance. He recommends that the scheduled increase in the employer contribution be suspended and that the increase in the employee tax be offset by an income tax credit. The resulting revenue loss to the system would be made good by transfer from general revenue. I have mixed feelings about this. For one thing, I note the underlying assumption that the employer-tax cut would be passed to the consumer—an assumption which runs counter to the standard position of the profession (though not mine) that both contributions are fully absorbed in wages. More important, I do not want to let the minor issue of next year's tax cut compromise the much more important one of how social security finance should be restructured in the longer run. Joe tends to view social security as part of the general problem of income maintenance. He, therefore, is quite happy to rely on general budgetary finance. I recognize that the system is on a pay-as-you-go basis, but nevertheless wish to retain and even strengthen its contractual nature. For this purpose I wish to keep the system distinct and as a separate unit. The payroll tax may not be the best source of finance, and its structure can be improved. However, the system should have its own source of finance, which is not to be touched in overall measures to lower or raise the level of taxation.[1]

I should end by noting a point of omission in Joe's paper. As he will readily agree, tax policies for the 1980s pose problems not only at the federal but also at the state and local levels. To note this aspect is in order, especially since Walter's debut as a public finance economist was in this field. If I remember correctly, it was in connection with Minnesota tax reform that he first entered the public arena. Moreover, the future of state–local taxation is closely related to that at the federal level. A nice question now before us is whether the problems of state and local finance are to be resolved by passing Proposition 13 and then turning to Washington for more revenue-sharing. The fathers of the Heller–Pechman plan might find themselves with an errant child, but this is another topic to be left for another day.

1. For a more detailed treatment, see my "Financing Social Security: A Reappraisal," *The Future of Social Security* (Cambridge, Mass.: MIT Press, 1981).

Providing Economic Advice to Government

Gardner Ackley *

Participating in this symposium in honor of Walter Heller is one of the most pleasant things that I have done in a long time. My admiration for Walter is truly unbounded. I had met him only once or twice before that day in April or May of 1962 when I picked up my telephone in Rome, Italy, to hear him ask if I would be willing and able to succeed Jim Tobin on the Council of Economic Advisers. But during the subsequent 2-1/2 years I came to know him exceedingly well. Indeed, much of that time we worked together 16 hours a day, 7 days a week. I can't remember his ever being impatient or unkind or ungrateful—to me or to anyone else. And I learned very much about how to convey economic ideas clearly, effectively, and interestingly. Of course I never learned to do it as well or as stylishly as he did and does.

Although I turned 65 a few months before he did, I will always look up to him as my mentor, my chairman, and—I hope—my friend. I am pleased and honored to participate in this symposium that honors him.

The topic assigned to me is the activity in which Walter made his mark as the most effective practitioner so far in American history: that of providing economic advice to government. However, Walter was not only a great

1. I am grateful to Paul Courant for extremely helpful comments on an earlier draft, and to Jeff Taylor for efficient research assistance.

practitioner of economic advising; he also wrote an excellent book about it. Indeed, between his book and Arthur Okun's, there is very little interesting or novel left for me to add.[2]

My favorite quotation on the subject of economists' advice to government is one attributed to Walter's close friend, the late Senator Hubert Humphrey, who is reported to have said: "We need a new, fresh, buoyant, forward-looking economics, to replace the tired old economics telling us we can't do the things we want to do—the things we have to do."[3]

It is not clear when this statement is supposed to have been made. One guess is that this is what Senator Humphrey told John Kennedy at Hyannisport a few weeks after the November 1960 election—and that it led to the choice of Walter Heller as chairman of the Council of Economic Advisers, and the birth of the "New Economics." I think that is a nice story. However, another version dates it about four years later, and identifies the recipient of the advice as Lyndon Johnson. This version proposes that it led to the replacement of the orthodox Walter Heller by Gardner Ackley—and thereby to the beginning of the Great Inflation. I don't really know which version is correct.

I don't even know that it's a genuine Humphreyism, although it surely sounds like Hubert. However, even if *he* didn't say it, surely many political figures must many times have said or thought things like that. For economists in government must very often tell their principals: "You can't do that."

2. Walter H. Heller, *New Dimensions of Political Economy* (Cambridge, Mass.: Harvard University Press, 1966), especially Chs. 1 and 2; Arthur M. Okun, *The Political Economy of Prosperity* (Brookings Institution 1970), especially Chs. 1 and 2.

3. As quoted by Martin Bronfenbrenner in the *Federal Reserve Bank of San Francisco Review*, December 1978.

In this election year it is painfully obvious—although it is also observable in every other year—that government needs more and better economic advice, or else that such advice needs to be more effectively and persuasively supplied. No other conclusion can be drawn from the paucity of permanent progress over the past twenty-five years in the quality of most government economic policies, in the economic content of party platforms, and in the recent economic declarations of presidents and presidential candidates. Clearly, economists—in and out of government—have provided insufficient, incorrect, or ineffective advice to government and to the political process more generally.

In thinking about whether and how this situation might be improved, I have chosen to give the topic a rather broader focus than merely a critique of organizational aspects of the Council of Economic Advisers, whose role and usefulness were so greatly magnified by the man whom we honor with this symposium, and whose advice did—at least for a time—seem to improve notably the quality of federal economic policies.

In its very broadest sense, the title that I have chosen for my paper could suggest fundamental and difficult questions about the nature and uses of economic knowledge— at least, about its uses for *public* purposes. What is the character of economic knowledge? To what extent, and for what purposes, does this knowledge ever support advice useful for government? You may see these deeper questions lurking in the background of some topics that I shall consider—perhaps in several. But I shall disregard them by merely assuming for purposes of my argument that economics *is* relevant, and *is* potentially useful in the formulation of public policy. Thus I wish only to consider how economic knowledge is best conveyed and brought to bear in governments' policy decisions.

I must at once narrow my discussion. Important as that is, I do not intend to discuss the appropriate manner of employment of the thousands of economists who do data collection, data processing, and analytical economic work in the administrative agencies, bureaus, and departments of the federal government. Their tasks and responsibilities relate mainly to policy administration, rather than to policy analysis and policy development. The same is broadly true for economists in state and local governments. Where this is *not* true, *some* of what I shall say about economists in the top layer of the federal government may also be relevant for them.

Economic Advice from Outside the Government

My first observation is that assuming, or concluding, that economic advice is relevant and potentially useful does not itself require that economists participate directly in policy formation. If we economists in academic and research institutions were doing our jobs satisfactorily—teaching our students, and researching, writing, and speaking on public issues—why would we ever need to leave our ivory towers and go to Washington? If we went at all, we would go only occasionally, and briefly, to consult or testify on specific important issues of public policy, or to participate in one-time commissions or studies. That way we would not need to ally ourselves in any but the most transient way with a particular party or partisan leader; we would avoid any implication that we approve—or perhaps have even helped to devise—every economic policy measure advocated by the party or leader that we may serve. Because we would *all* remain free to criticize, parties and their leaders might even have to moderate—at least somewhat—their apparent propensities to advocate absurd doctrines and to adopt worthless or damaging policies.

This is indeed the stance that the great majority of economists prefer to take—or at least prefer to *appear to take*. But it is too often a mere appearance. For most economists never bother to inform themselves sufficiently on public economic issues to be able to comment on them intelligently, or at least relevantly. Such policy comment as they may have typically consists of incoherent and uninformed grumblings to their colleagues about the idiocy of politicians, flashes of ironic rhetoric in their lectures to students, or the manipulation in journal articles of simplistic models that purport to prove how wrong certain complex policies are—or how right some other quite simplistic policy would be.

There are, of course, important exceptions: There have been and are economists who never formally participate in government, but who feel an urgent responsibility to provide, from the outside, informed and relevant professional comment on a wide range of public economic issues, and in a context and format that can reach policymakers. The currently outstanding example of this posture is probably Paul Samuelson: in my view not merely the most brilliant economic analyst, but also the most effective economic educator—in the broadest sense—of our era. No one else comes close. However, there are a fair number of others who, like Paul, have never served in government (or at least not yet), who take policy questions seriously, and who feel a responsibility to provide intelligible professional advice from outside the government. They include economists as diverse as Milton Friedman, Franco Modigliani, Martin Feldstein, Lawrence Klein, Alan Meltzer, Robert Lekachman, and many others. They are too few, perhaps, but a sizable number.

There are others who *have* at one time or another (or several times) served in government, and who feel a responsibility to remain informed, and to comment from the outside on the main economic issues of government policy—in speeches to professional and nonprofessional groups, in the press, or in congressional testimony—in some detail and in language designed to be both intelligible and persuasive to layman and politician. The man whom we honor by this symposium—along with the late Arthur Okun—is surely the outstanding example of that class of former government participants who continue to advise from outside; but there are many others, somewhat less remarkable, including quite a few of us who are here today.

I should add, too, that there are *nonacademic* economists, some of them even nameless, who contribute useful and relevant information and comment on public policies in commercial publications that are sometimes highly professional in quality. An outstanding example, of course, is Leonard Silk. Also, for example, there are the anonymous authors of the *Monthly Morgan Guaranty Survey* and the companion *World Financial Markets*, the only "bank letters" that I find to be of consistently professional quality.

Highly professional economic advice is also provided to governments, in depth and detail, through independent research institutions, of which The Brookings Institution, The American Enterprise Institute for Public Policy Research, the Rand Corporation, and Data Resources, Inc. are prominent examples. Large private-interest organizations of many kinds, as well as large business firms, which have permanent staffs containing professional economists, also freely proffer economic advice, often backed up by economic analysis of varying quality, ranging from sometimes excellent (for example, in the case of the CED) to worthless.

To be sure, there are many limitations on the quality and usefulness of the economic advice that comes from outside the government. Although it is clearly not the case for those whose names I have mentioned, the economist's frequent tendency toward *oversimplification*, one's *self-selection* for the role of public adviser, the *implicit competition* among outsiders for a hearing, and perhaps the encouragement of their newspaper or magazine editors or their speakers' bureaus, may sometimes engender a trace (or maybe more than a trace) of the same irresponsibility that we deplore in political figures. But this is no reason to discourage serious and relevant advising from outside government by able economists. On the contrary, we need a great deal more of it.

The Contribution of Participant Advisers

Nevertheless, the advice governments receive from outside can never replace the need for full-time participant advisers within the government. This is because the most useful and effective advice can best be tendered within the context of the political, bureaucratic, and administrative settings in which the important economic issues arise. This does not depend on the insider having significantly better information than the outsider—he doesn't. Nor is it because the insider has more time to think—quite the contrary. It is because 1) the insider's advice is likely to be received more favorably by the political leader, and 2) because the insider's advice is likely to be better and more effective advice.

Why is it received more favorably? Not all political leaders are as suspicious and sensitive as was Lyndon Johnson, who (and possibly with reason) saw a potential Judas in each of his associates with whom he had worked less than ten years—or preferably twenty. But even a less paranoic leader surely has greater confidence in advice that comes from persons who have become familiar and who have demonstrated both their effectiveness and their trustworthiness. You may say that the politician should be concerned only with the quality of the ideas and advice that he receives, whatever their source; but the very reason that he needs economic advice (and other highly technical kinds) is his own inability to understand and to resolve technical problems without such professional assistance. Thus he is unable adequately to judge the quality of the policy ideas that he receives from outside, without his own inside adviser's help. Moreover, the fact that he can readily ask questions of the participant adviser, seek explanations, raise objections and have them directly answered makes his inside adviser enormously more useful.

Furthermore, the political leader normally wishes to be able to try out ideas, discuss his options, and prepare his plans in private, without tipping off his political opponents or private interests that might benefit or be hurt by his proposals. He cannot be assured of confidentiality unless his economic (as well as his other) advisers are *inside participants*—and, of course, not always even then. Moreover, although the economist may consider it silly, the political leader often desires to enhance the interest in his proposals by their surprise announcement; or he wishes to create the illusion that they are of his own devising; or he seeks to flatter the supporters (or potential opponents) of his policies by giving them advance notice and a usually meaningless opportunity to comment. Indeed, his ability to orchestrate the unveiling of his initiatives may very well be a significant ingredient in their potential political success. This is not to say that premeditated leaks that certain options are under consideration may not also at times be a constructive instrument of political leadership—

also widely used. But the successful political leader needs the opportunity to control the time and manner in which his initiatives reach the public—and even the time and manner in which they reach many of his associates in government. None of these is assured if he must depend on the discretion of outside experts.[4]

Why is inside advice better and more effective? Writing on the subject "Economists in Government,"[5] Sir Alec Cairncross reminds us that Jacob Viner once said: "The list of handicaps of the economist theorist as participant in the formulation of public policy is discouragingly long." To be sure, we may comfort ourselves (as we do at the end of each semester) by reflecting that the effective transmission of economic understanding depends not only on the attributes of the transmitter but also on the intellect and desire to learn of the intended recipient. And public officials are mostly just our students grown older; many of them still can't or won't learn. We must admit, however, that the content of our message is usually not as clear and simple to the political leader as it seems to us to be. Cairncross also quotes Lionel Robbins (who, at the time he wrote it, was the top British economic advisor, as Director of the Economic Section of the British Treasury). According to Robbins:

> Economics, at any rate that branch of economics which is most applicable in practice, is not a difficult subject in the sense in which, say, mathematical physics is difficult. The most useful economic principles, when stated in their most general form, seem often mere banalities, almost an anti-climax after the formidable controversies amid which they have evolved. Yet experience seems

4. There may also be good *economic* reasons for holding advice and discussion confidential until a public release date. On this, see G. P. Schultz and K. W. Dam, *Economic Policy Behind the Headlines* (New York: Norton, 1977), pp. 9, 10.

5. *Lloyds Bank Review*, no. 95, January 1970, pp. 1–18.

to show that, without systematic training in the application of such platitudes, the most acute minds are liable to go astray; the economist, if he is humble, is heir to perpetual surprises, as he witnesses the incredible muddles which continually emerge from lay discussions of these matters.

Cairncross comments on Robbins' remark:

> This is part of the truth, but part only. For one has to admit that the laymen who might be led astray by intellectual muddle are not necessarily much better off if they are marched in bold logic by the priestly up the garden path. Economists may avoid muddle only to fall into other traps baited to catch the theoretician: Excessive abstraction, disregard for inconvenient facts, unwarranted assumptions. . . .
>
> The case for increasing the number of senior economists in government service is not assisted by representing economists as supermen able to transform the economy by technical wizardry and rendering administrators and ministers alike redundant. Anyone who talks in these terms has never been present at the kind of discussion between economists, administrators and ministers at which it is by no means uncommon for the economists to talk politics, the administrators to talk economics, and ministers to discuss administrative complications. An outsider might have great difficulty in deciding who, among those present, was a professional economist and would be very unlikely to conclude that an economist, as such, was in a particularly powerful position in debating most issues of economic policy.[6]

In short, the policymakers whom economists advise have to be concerned with the *political problems* involved in getting a policy adopted and with its *political consequences* if it is. The economists who advise them, therefore, cannot avoid considering the political aspects of economic policy. And both the politician and the economist must be aware of the *administrative problems* raised by the effort to make economic policy effective.

6. Cairncross, *Lloyds Bank Review*, pp. 6, 7.

To be sure, the economist must take great care as to the manner and the extent to which he gets involved in the politics of acceptance; and there are many things that he does not know about the functioning of bureaucracies. Yet he does have important contributions to make on both the political and administrative aspects. The notion is absurdly oversimplified that the economic adviser can or does merely present to his principal a menu listing the economic consequences of each of a variety of policy options, leaving it to administrators to design each option, and to politicians to evaluate and select the preferred set of consequences. The adviser does not perform his duty when he merely provides a detailed description of each of the estimated consequences—and a measure of the variance of each estimate—of a reduction of gasoline consumption, or of deaths from industrial accidents, or of the rate of inflation, by 1 percent, 5 percent, or 15 percent, leaving it to administrative experts to choose the best way to achieve each reduction, and leaving it to the politician's "objective function" (or that of his political party or faction) to decide which set of uncertain costs and consequences maximizes his (or their) utility.

This concept is grossly oversimplified because the design of methods to achieve each possible reduction often involves economic choices of substantial gravity, choices on which economists have substantial expertise (for example, the choice among particular direct or indirect economic incentives and various forms of command).[7] It is also oversimplified because the policymaker rarely if ever has a clear notion of his objective (or loss) function and has never tried to pose his choices in those terms. Moreover, he has no idea how to evaluate the measures of uncertainty

7. On this, see Charles L. Schultze, *The Public Use of Private Interest* (Brookings, 1977).

attached to each set of outcomes. The economist can and must help the political leader to evaluate the menu of choices in terms of the leader's political value system. [8] This is not easy to do. It involves what Richard G. Lipsey refers to as problems of *translation*:

> ... When the advisor wishes to communicate with the lay decision maker he must *translate* from the technical jargon to the vernacular. The technical expert must do the translation because he knows both languages while the lay decision maker does not. But translation is an art ... [and] there is no one best translation from positive economic knowledge as expressed by economists to the vernacular used by lay persons, and any one translation will produce one reaction from policy maker A and quite another from policy maker B. ... There is no escaping it: the economic advisor and the policy maker are in a complex human relation entangled in various uncertainties and communicating with each other through an inevitable haze of emotional reactions. Economists may strive towards an ideal of communicating what is known and unknown as objectively as possible. But like virtue and charity, objectivity remains an ideal that guides our actions, not a reality that fully describes them. [9]

George Schultz said much the same thing more colorfully, speaking to economists about his experiences in government:

> When I first came to Washington I used to think that there were two kinds of people: substantive folks, like you and me, who

8. I like to add that, as a concerned citizen, with his own value system, the advisor has a right—or perhaps a duty—to express his own preference, so long as he makes it clear that it involves value judgments, and explains the values that influenced his choice. I have developed this point in "The Contribution of Economists to Policy Formation," *Journal of Finance*, XXI, May 1966, pp. 169–177; and in "The Role of the Economist as Policy Advisor in the United States," in *Essays in Honour of Giuseppe Ugo Papi*, CEDAM, Padova, vol. II, 1973, pp. 9–24.

9. R. G. Lipsey, "Economists, Policy Makers, and Economic Policy," Discussion Paper no. 334, Institute for Economic Research, Queen's University, March 1976, pp. 6, 7.

analyze problems and propose optimal solutions; and the politicians who do their thing, for good or for ill, with the proposals we
make. I never had a sillier idea. One cannot make, much less
implement, effective policies without taking political and bureaucratic factors into account and, on occasion, turning them to
advantage.[10]

There are, of course, cases in which problems of commu-
nication between economist and policymaker never arise:
when the economic policymaker is himself an economist.
One thinks of Robert Roosa, George Schultz, John
Dunlop, Ray Marshall, Alfred Kahn, Barry Bosworth, a
succession of budget directors in the 1960s and a fair
number of governors of the Federal Reserve. During World
War II, economists occupied many major administrative
positions in the war agencies, e.g., J. K. Galbraith, Robert
Nathan, Charles Kindleberger. Abroad one thinks of
Harold Wilson or Luigi Einaudi. If they have economists
on their staffs, they have no trouble communicating. But
when the administrator-economist advises *his* superior—
e.g., when George Schultz advised Gerald Ford—he had the
same communications problems that Alan Greenspan did.

Models of Organization for Economic Policy Advice

I have argued that economic advising—by participant
advisers, within the government—is a necessary, although
difficult, function. How then can it best be organized?

The best way to organize the provision of economic
advice at the highest levels of government clearly depends
very much on the structure of that government, and on the

10. G. Schultz, "Reflections on Political Economy" (excerpts from an address to a joint meeting of the American Economic Association and the American Finance Association, December 28, 1973), *Challenge: The Magazine of
Economic Affairs*, March–April 1974, p. 10.

character of its economic policies. The best way will be different in a parliamentary than in a presidential system; it may differ considerably depending on whether government intervention is primarily accomplished through demand-management policies or through more direct measures (e.g., "indicative planning"); the extent and character of the use of incomes policy may also make a difference, and so will the institutions and traditions of the country's civil service.

This means that an organizational scheme that seems to work well in one country might not work at all in another; surely, no operating plan is directly transferable from one to another. But neither is a particular manner of organization deterministically tied to a particular form of government; and government forms are themselves subject to constant evolution. The Council of Economic Advisers was a specific social invention, as was the Congressional Budget Office; there can be others. And we may pick up some good ideas by looking at how other countries do it.

In thinking and learning about the ways in which various countries organize their provision of economic advice at the highest level of government, I have been struck by their variety. Let me list and briefly *characterize* six basic models:

1) The U.S. Council of Economic Advisers—its personnel *academic, temporary, visible, political* (in the sense that its top people normally serve only in an administration of a particular party); and its operations *centralized*; working, of course, in conjunction with top civil servants and political administrators in the White House, the Treasury, the OMB, and elsewhere.

2) The U.S. Congressional Budget Office—its personnel *professional, permanent, nonpolitical,* largely *invisible,* and *centralized*; working with the entirely

political membership of Congress, and the mainly political congressional staffs.

3) The German Council of Economic Experts—its personnel *academic, slowly rotating, nonpolitical, highly visible*, and *centralized*; set up to advise the government, but working entirely independently of the government.[11]

4) The United Kingdom's top economic civil service—its personnel nominally *permanent* (although with substantial turnover), *nonpolitical, invisible or nearly so*, and largely *dispersed* in the ministries and departments.[12] Although some are professionals, or come from academic careers, until recently the majority were not. Still, one recognizes Robbins and Cairncross, whom I have already mentioned, as not only professionals, but academics—along with Keynes, Henry Clay, I. M. D. Little, Thomas Balogh, and Nicholas Kaldor.

5) In Japan, high-level economic advice emanates from the top layers of a *permanent* and *dispersed* civil service, within which administrative and analytical-advisory roles are usually not sharply segregated, with particular

---

11. The best reference on the German Council is still Henry Wallich, "The American Council of Economic Advisers and the German *Sachverstaendigenrat:* A Study in the Economics of Advice," *Quarterly Journal of Economics*, vol. 82, August, 1968, pp. 349–79. However, see also Paul Malles, *Economic Consultative Bodies: Their Origins and Institutional Characteristics* (Economic Council of Canada, 1971), pp. 163–91; and Herbert Giersch, "Macroeconomic Policy in West Germany" in *Economic Planning and Macroeconomic Policy* (Papers and Proceedings of a Conference held by the Japan Economic Research Center, September 1970), vol. I, pp. 32–50; and *A Discussion with Herbert Giersch* (American Enterprise Institute, AEI Studies 147, 1977).

12. It is not entirely clear how much turnover there really is. See A. W. Coats, "Economists in Government: A Research Field for the Historian of Economics," *History of Political Economy*, vol. 10, Summer 1978, especially pp. 304–305; Sir Alec Cairncross, "Economists in Government," *Lloyds Bank Review*, no. 95, January 1970, especially pp. 15–17. On the general topic of economic advice in Britain, see also Sir Robert Hall, "The Place of the Economist in Government"; *Oxford Economic Papers*, June 1955, pp. 119–35, and "Reflections on the Practical Application of Economics," *Economic Journal*, vol. 69, December 1959, pp. 639–52; and the references in footnote 15.

individuals rotating frequently among such roles, before ultimately moving out into top-level political or business careers. Members of this group are professionals, but not professional economists. This Japanese model is quite unique and probably nontransferable.

6) There are several countries in which the most important economic advice is centered in an agency with mainly indicative-planning and perhaps incomes-policy responsibilities (e.g., France, Netherlands, Belgium, and Canada), where a permanent, apolitical economic analysis group, often of high professional quality (e.g., Tinbergen), typically serves, or participates in, a policy council that is "representative" of the broad economic interest groups. This model, too, is probably of little relevance for the United States.[13]

In addition to these six *basic models*, let me also list six *auxiliary models* of organization for economic advice that might supplement (but could not replace) any one of the types just described. They include the following:

1) The use of slowly rotating bodies of part-time confidential economic consultants from outside government (mostly, but not exclusively, academic), as, for example, at times, by the U.S. Secretary of the Treasury, and by the Board of Governors of the Federal Reserve System.

2) The use of National-Academy-type panels of experts, assigned to investigate and report, privately or publicly, on a single, specific, major issue.

3) The use of *ad hoc*, temporary public commissions, with an *ad hoc*, temporary staff, to study a particular economic problem. Such a commission is likely to contain prominent economists and to be served by a staff

13. See P. Malles, *Economic Consultive Bodies*, chs. 1, 2, 3; and, for Canada, see also R. W. Phidd and G. Bruce Doern, *The Politics and Management of Canadian Economic Policy* (Macmillan of Canada, 1978).

containing academic or research economists. In both the United States and the United Kingdom, such commissions have often made major educational contributions, even though their specific recommandations may have been largely or totally ignored.

4) Particular problems or questions may be contracted out to consulting organizations, profit or nonprofit, for analysis and advice. As we all know, there is a wide range in the quality of such advice, from excellent to awful.

5) The staffs of congressional committees, and even of individual senators and representatives, now contain substantial numbers of economists, of varying quality and of varying degrees of use and of usefulness.

6) Finally, in countries with a central bank independent of the government (of which the United States is the purest case), we ordinarily find a quite independent and separately organized provision of economic advice to the bank, mostly by its own permanent staff.

Thus in the United States, we have the unique and glorious situation of three quite independent provisions of inside professional economic advice to the top levels of the federal government: to the President and his administration; to the Congress; and to the Federal Reserve. Lest you should find that somewhat appalling, take comfort in the fact that economics is an exact science and value-free; its every proposition has already been proved either correct or incorrect; new knowledge accrues daily, and the only problem is to keep up with its accrual. Since it is all pure science, the same advice must be proffered by the three sets of advisers as would be the case were there a single set!

Characteristics of Alternative Organizational Forms

In describing the several models of organization for economic advice, I have used certain pairs of adjectives to compare or to contrast their character; let me comment briefly on the dichotomies suggested by these adjectives, and suggest the advantages or disadvantages that each characteristic may bring to the effectiveness of public economic policy. (I ignore the auxiliary models.)

I have little to say about one pair of adjectives that I used in describing my models: centralized versus dispersed. The total economics staff of every government is, of course, widely dispersed, as are even the top advisers in Britain and Japan—as is likely to be the case in a parliamentary system.[14] In the United States, economic advising is dispersed (as I noted earlier) among the three major sources of power in economic affairs, the executive branch, the Congress, and the Federal Reserve. Within the executive branch, participation in *top-level* economic advising has probably become somewhat more dispersed than it used to be (as I will discuss a bit later); in addition, of course, thousands of economists are dispersed throughout the executive and legislative branches.

I recall proposals in the past to construct more formal ties between the Council and the economic staffs of Labor, Commerce, and the other major agencies. I have also heard the argument that the Council's staff economists would do more good if they were dispersed among the operating departments and agencies. My own view is that neither of these changes merits consideration; either one would not only reduce the effectiveness of the Council as adviser

14. To be sure, there has been some degree of organizational centralization of British economists: during World War II, in the Economic Section of the Cabinet Office; later in the Economic Section of the Treasury; still later in the Government Economic Service. Yet it is my impression that the earlier appearance of centralization really reflected the near-absence of any use of economists outside the Cabinet Office or Treasury; and that the subsequent centralization has been largely for administrative rather than operational purposes.

to the President, but reduce the total usefulness of economists in the federal government.

As a second pair of adjectives, I described the personnel
of some of my organizational models as "academic" or
"professional," the personnel of others as their opposites.
Both Sir Alec Cairncross and Prof. I. M. D. Little, who
have written about their experiences as participant economic advisers in Britain, tended somewhat to derogate
the professional aspects of the adviser's job.[15] However, on
balance, each concluded that professional training is
indeed important for the government adviser, although
never quite describing the essence of this training other
than that it centers around economic theory. I agree, and
I thus use the term "professional" to describe a person

15. Little writes: "Before I became an economic adviser I found it rather
hard to understand why economists were likely to be useful (except in rather
limited ways). It seemed to me that the basic essential framework of applic-
able ideas was so simple and limited that any able man concerned with economic affairs could and would acquire them as he went along, without any need
of formal training. As soon as one strayed beyond this very limited corpus of
thought, economic theory became inapplicable. And as for any really professional methods of prediction—well, any sensible economist regards them as ex-
ploratory exercises in method rather than as something to be trusted in practice." ("The Economist in Whitehall," *Lloyds Bank Review*, no. 44, April
1957, p. 35.)
Carincross suggests that "it is reasonable to ask whether an academic training in economics is indispensable to an economic adviser or whether it is not
more important to find a man with the right gifts and trust him to work out
the theory for himself. To a mature and experienced man with an eye for the
ways of the world there is nothing very abstruse about economic theory: certainly not about those parts of economic theory that are truly operational and
bear on the real dilemmas of policy. It is arguable that the economic theory
that is taught always relates to the problems of an earlier decade or even an
earlier generation and that it is left to administrators to recognize the new
problems as they emerge, grapple with them and subdue them with such theoretical tools as they can fashion." ("On Being an Economic Adviser," *Scottish
Journal of Political Economy*, vol. II, no. 3, October 1955, p. 183.)
On the other hand, P. D. Henderson argues (again in the British case) that
the scarcity of professionally trained economists in government decision-
making has produced disastrous results in Britain. See his "The Use of Economists in British Administration," *Oxford Economic Papers*, N.S. 13, 1961,
pp. 5-26.

systematically trained in economic theory. However, systematic training in quantitative analysis is equally essential, since the questions that political leaders ask their advisers are only occasionally "whether or not" but ordinarily take the form "how much."

Nevertheless, in considering what it means to call an economic adviser a "professional," I remind you of the top-level Japanese civil servant (especially in the Ministry of Finance or of International Trade and Industry, where the most crucial economic policies originate). He graduated close to the top of his class, preferably at Tokyo University (or at one of a few others); he had no graduate university training in economics (perhaps not even undergraduate training). Rather, he was trained "on the job" to perform both high-level economic analysis as well as the wide variety of other professional and administrative tasks among which he rotates. Shall we call him a "professional"? Certainly not when he entered the government; even by the time that he has reached a top advisory role, he is a generalist, not an economist; and he is certainly not an "academic."

American economists who have served as senior economic advisers and have written about their experiences—in particular, Walter Heller and Arthur Okun—have taken a very positive view of the relevance and usefulness of the academic–professional attributes that they and their associates brought to their employment. And, so far as the United States is concerned, there has not up to now appeared to be any alternative to the recruitment of most senior economic advisers from academic backgrounds—although the cases of Council members Leon Keyserling, Alan Greenspan, George Eads, and Lyle Gramley mark partial exceptions to my rule; several highly effective members of the Council's senior staff also have not been academics—David Lusher comes to mind as a prime example.

A third pair of adjectives that I used to describe alternative models of economic advisory organization was the "temporary–permanent" contrast. And this turns out to be closely associated with two other contrasting attributes: "political–apolitical"; and "visible–invisible." Given the facts that most really top American economists are academics and that academics are unwilling to remain indefinitely in the government, it is probably not useful to pursue the temporary–permanent dichotomy very far. However, CEA experience surely suggests some particular advantages of a personnel that is essentially both academic and temporary, both for top advisors and their senior staff. One is their willingness to work incredibly long and hard—punishment that could not be endured were the positions permanent. A second is the independence that derives from a permanent career elsewhere—to which one can and will return if proffered advice is habitually ignored, or if asked to prostitute professional reputation for political ends. A third advantage is the continuing flow of personnel with fresh ideas, new research techniques, and knowledge of the latest research results. (This is matched only by the advantage to the universities and research institutions as the advisers return with renewed inventories of relevant issues on which research is needed.) The prime disadvantage of the constant turnover of advisory personnel is, of course, the repeated and substantial cost of learning the ropes. Neither these advantages nor the disadvantage accrue in the Japanese or British civil-service models; nor for senior economic advisers in the U.S. Congressional Budget Office, or in the Federal Reserve.

In a political system in which one set of "rascals" is frequently turned out for another, any degree of permanence for senior U.S. economic advisers would, of course, require that they also be apolitical and relatively invisible. To be sure, the legislation creating the Council of Economic Advisers does not require that they be visible and political; the invisible Dr. Nourse could well have served in a Republican administration, and the barely visible Arthur Burns of 1956 might have survived in a Democratic one.

Of course, invisibility for the U.S. economic adviser would mean his inability to occupy any piece of the "bully pulpit" (as Teddy Roosevelt described the American presidency). He would lose his opportunity to educate not merely the president and his inner circle, but the entire nation: the job that Walter Heller performed so superbly. This is surely a part of the attraction of the job for many of the confirmed academics who take education seriously.

In order for economic advisers to be *both* apolitical *and* visible seems to require an arrangement like that of the German Council of Economic Experts—which surely has much to recommend it from the standpoint of many academic economists. I am myself unable to judge whether the German economists who have served in the Council of Experts might have made a greater contribution to German polity had they served *within* the government; but I believe that it is a quite legitimate question. However, it would have been a very different kind of service.

With the rapidly growing employment of highly trained and talented American economists in business, banking, contract-research organizations, and in staff positions in government itself, it is at least conceivable that the top economic-advisory roles in the U.S. government might someday come to be filled, not by academics on leave, but by more permanent, nonacademic professionals—some of whom might even come to serve presidents of both parties. That would require a considerable evolution of the role of the Council of Economic Advisers, making it far less visible and less political—but not necessarily less professional. Yet it is not beyond the realm of possibility.

One could even imagine that a completely nonpolitical Council of Economic Advisers could replace the need for separate economic advisory organizations to the administration, the Congress, and the Federal Reserve. A "Supreme Court of Economics," it could be consulted by all three; or it could issue, on its own initiative, analyses of current economic problems and their possible resolutions, which president, Congress, and the Federal Reserve could take account of in their policy decisions.

If one speculates on how such an arrangement might evolve from our existing machinery for economic advice, one might suppose the CBO to be its most likely ancestor. And somewhere along the evolutionary chain one might suppose that its present director would have become a committee or council. But who would select the members of this supreme committee or council? Who would decide whether it would consist of the equivalent of Meltzer, Feldstein, and Boskin, rather than of Perry, Thurow, and Blinder? Or would the choice be of some combination of scholars whose policy views were much less predictable because they had never been interested in policy questions? But would those economists want that job? Or would they be the most appropriate advisers? I doubt it.

And who would select them? In Germany, the Council of Economic Experts is appointed by the President of the Republic—an aloof, respected figure (or figurehead) uninvolved in current political wars. Presumably he acts on the advice of university rectors, and of the presidents of learned societies. But we have no such figure to make the appointments, unless he were the chief justice of the Supreme Court.

Even the briefest consideration should also convince almost anyone that, however distinguished the Supreme Court of Economics, the President would still seek his own economic advisers, as would Congress and its individual members, and as would the Federal Reserve, Such a politically neutral (or neuter) council could thus mainly constitute an addition to, rather than a substitute for, present machinery for the provision of economic advice. That doesn't mean that it would be a bad idea; indeed, Arther Okun once suggested such a second council of advisers.[16]

However, for the present we must make do with our existing system, and I now turn to ways in which its effectiveness might be improved.

Improving the Organizational Effectiveness of U.S. Economic Advice

It is a dozen years since I have had any significant association with economic advising the United States. Thus my only information about recent problems and changes in its organization and operations comes from scanty references in public sources. I know even less about how the changing character of U.S. economic problems may have exposed weaknesses in the system, or about how the personal and institutional roles of advisers have responded to the backgrounds, personalities, and operating modes of the last three Presidents. Thus I have little confidence in the relevance or usefulness of the comments that I will make on organizational matters.

I am sure, however, that it has continued to be the case that the Council of Economic Advisers is not the President's sole source of economic advice. A number of other senior members of each administration have had their own channels to the President; most of them have their own

16. It should be recognized, however, that, if such a council were to be representative of the current broad range of professional opinion—as it undoubtedly should be—it could provide a convincing majority view on, at most, a limited number of major current policy issues.

staff economists, and support their policy recommendations by some kind of economic analysis. The extent of
the influence that each one has had depends, ultimately,
on the quality and usefulness of his advice and the extent
to which it is consonant with the President's own values
and perceptions. In that competition, I am sure that, since
1968 as well as before, there have been many occasions
when the Council's advice has been preferred (when it
differed from that of other senior advisers) and times when
it has not.

However, the effectiveness of the Council depends not
merely on the quality of its advice and the President's
susceptibilities, but to some extent on the nature and
effectiveness of its own organization and that of the President's office and of the various modes of access to his
attention. Despite my unfamiliarity with recent events, my
subject calls for comment on these organizational matters.
I will arrange them under three headings. The first deals
with the council itself.

Organization and Responsibilities
of the Council of Economic Advisers

As I left the Council in February 1968, I had one major
and overriding concern about the Council's own organization. It related to the operational responsibilities that the
Council then carried for the conduct of the government's
incomes policy. Efforts to delegate any significant part of
that activity to the Departments of Commerce and Labor
had proved fruitless—as we all feared that they would.

The institution by the Nixon administration of the
independent Council on Wage and Price Stability
(COWPS), and its continuance to the present time, sup-
ports my view that a separate agency is the only feasible
way to administer a U.S. incomes policy—at least, in the
absence of a Department of Economic Affairs, which, for a

number of reasons, I favored then and still do.[17] I am not at all sure, however, that the organizational arrangements relating COWPS to the president's office and to the council are appropriate. In particular, I am unclear about the usefulness of the president's Special Assistant on Inflation. However, I do not know enough about the present arrangement, nor its functioning, to comment usefully. Clearly, COWPS cannot report directly to the President; having it report through the Council would again immerse the Council in incomes-policy administration. A Department of Economic Affairs (if it existed) would clearly be the place for it to report.

Other than incomes-policy activities, very little else appears to have changed over the past twenty years or more in the size, character, or organization of the Council. This, in itself, seems to confirm my own judgment in 1968 that there were no other significant problems requiring reoganization or restructuring of the Council.[18]

17. This was a recommendation of President Johnson's Task Force on Government Organization, headed by Ben Heineman. The "Heineman Commission" was appointed in 1966, and apparently reported informally to the president in June 1967. Its "Final Report," of which I recently obtained a copy, is dated September 15, 1967. President Johnson neither released the report nor permitted its transmission to the Nixon administration. (See L. Berman, *The Office of Management and Budget and the Presidency, 1921–1979.* Princeton: Princeton University Press, 1979, pp. 85–90.) Such a department would, of course, inevitably affect the role of the Council of Economic Advisers.

18. At one time during my term as chairman I was intrigued with the possibility of establishing a modest research facility that would be attached to the council, but insulated completely from day-to-day activities. Many former members of the Council's staff have complained that they never had time to do any serious research on problems assigned to them because they were continually given assignments with 24- or 36-hour deadlines. A number and variety of such complaints were voiced by former staff members in interviews conducted by Professor W. R. Allen. (See his "Economics, Economists, and Economic Policy: Modern American Experiences," *History of Political Economy*, vol. 9, Spring 1977, pp. 48–88.) At the time, I was talked out of my proposal by my colleagues; however, rereading Allen's piece in preparing this paper has again raised in my mind the possibility that a physically separate and protected research staff of, say, 20 economists might have considerable merit. Each would be assigned to do research on current and anticipated policy issues in an area assigned to him, but would be protected from involvement in current activities and controversies. The problem is that those who were doing good and useful work would inevitably get involved. The others would contribute little.

Relationships of the Council of Economic Advisers
to the President and His Administration

The problems here to be considered concern the
council's relationships to the president; his staff; the other
former "Troika" agencies, OMB and Treasury; and an
outer ring of departments and agencies concerned with
economic matters.

In the Carter administration, the Departments of
Labor and Commerce have finally achieved their long-
desired participation in the periodic assessment and
forecasting exercise, now formally chaired by the Council. And, since the responsibility for the policy recommendations that used to follow from each Troika forecast
appears also to have been transferred to a larger body,
the Troika apparently no longer exists – at least
formally.

Instead, since the early 1970s, recommendations regarding economic policy—both macroeconomic and other—
have been made to the President by an intermediary
formal policy committee, consisting of the heads of several
departments and agencies in addition to the former Troika
agencies, along with members of the President's staff.
From the public record, I discern only modest differences
among the Nixon administration's "Council on Economic
Policy," the Ford administration's "Economic Policy
Board," and the Carter administration's "Economic Policy
Group"—the latter two equipped with a smaller "Executive Committee." In each of these groups, the council
chairman is only one of a number of senior advisers on
economic affairs. There is nothing new about that, of
course. Yet the organizational change *could* mean a substantial change in the council's role, and in the extent,
nature, and quality of the professional economic advice
that the president receives.

One possible *advantage* that I can see in a formal intermediary economic policy council, board, or group is that, to the extent that *all* important economic policy recommendations, from all parts of the President's administration, flow through this committee, the Council may be better enabled to discover, to have time to evaluate, and to find allies who might support its opposition to proposed policy actions originating in any part of the administration that are inadequately supported by professional economic analysis.

I can see no obvious disadvantage in such an intermediary committee—whether called a "council," a "board," or a "group"—provided that certain conditions are met. One such condition is that the Council is considered to be the professional economic adviser not merely *to the committee* but *to the President,* and that the Council retains and actively uses its direct channel to the President. A second condition is that the chairman of the policy council, board, or group is only a *chairman* (as some have reported that George Schultz was), rather than a deputy president for economic affairs (as some have reported that John Connally was—or sought to be). A third condition is that *all* major proposals for economic policy—*including those originating in the White House itself*—are reviewed in the same way by the committee, and come to the President for decision in the same way.

I do not know, of course, whether or to what extent my three conditions are satisfied or violated. However, in his brilliant but extremely pessimistic analysis of recent economic policymaking, "Re-establishing an Economic Consensus: An Impossible Agenda,"[19] Barry Bosworth is not very reassuring. He writes that "The Domestic Policy

19. *Daedulus: Journal of the American Academy of Arts and Sciences,* Summer 1980, pp. 59–70.

Staff [of the White House], which had once served as a
broker between different agencies, the economic advisers,
and the political advisers, was expanded in the Carter
Administration to become still another center of policy
initiatives." Given the direct access of the White House
staff to the President—inevitably more direct than that of
the CEA—this would appear to be a dangerous development for rational economic policymaking. It would not be
less dangerous if the domestic policy staff contained its
own professional economists.

I will have to depend on those more familiar with
recent government operations to reassure me—or to confirm my fears—regarding the organizational changes of
recent years. However, Bosworth's comments are
disturbing:

> As a result [of these changes], the President today is confronted
> with a minimum of five and often as many as ten sources of expert
> advice. With neither the mechanism nor the incentive for forcing a
> consensus, he is often compelled to choose between sharply
> divergent views. Yet no advisor feels personally responsible, nor is
> it possible to hold him accountable for the outcome of a decision;
> he can always argue, and very plausibly, that the resulting overall
> policy was certainly not his own.[20]

This certainly did not—in my memory—occur under the
Troika arrangement.

Bosworth goes on to argue that the fault lies not entirely
with organizational arrangements. He lays it in part to the
strength of rival interest groups in our society, in part to
"a President [who is] not driven by any overriding
economic philosophy of his own but approaches each issue
with an open-minded willingness to hear all sides and to do
the best thing in every case," in part to the "cacophony
of contradictory recommendations emerging from the

---

20. B. Bosworth, "Re-establishing an Economic Consensus," p. 66.

community of 'expert economic opinion'," and to a decline in the quality and experience of government personnel at all levels. It is a devastating indictment, and it includes the economics profession.

From this distance—both in time, and in contemporary contact—I am able neither personally to confirm Bosworth's indictment nor to propose remedies. At one time, shortly after leaving the government, and reflecting on the threats to the Council in the development of a strong and aggressive White House domestic policy staff, I floated to some former colleagues proposals for reorganizing the relationship of council to president that included the idea that the council chairman would acquire a second title, as Special Assistant to the President for Economic Affairs—rather like the Special Assistant to the President for National Security Affairs, who is also chairman of the National Security Council. I was talked out of this by Arthur Okun and others who felt that it was a bad idea. And I have come increasingly to see how right they were. The special assistant's role is basically incompatible with the council chairman's role as a professional economic adviser; one probably could not do both.[21]

The Council's Relationships with the Rest of Government

This heading is needed for completeness; however, I have little to offer on the organizational relationships of the Council to the Congress, the Federal Reserve System, and the other independent agencies.

---

21. I have been reminded of this by reading Berman's *The Office of Management and Budget and the Presidency, 1921–1979.* Much of his book concerns the inconsistency between the role of budget director, as the manager of a professional analysis staff, and the role of a White House staff assistant with responsibility for policy development.

I assume that mutually useful professional contacts have developed between the Council and an organization established after my time in government—the Congressional Budget Office—with an abundant flow of ideas and analyses in both directions. With respect to the Congress itself, the tradition has apparently been maintained that the Council testifies only on major policy matters, mostly macroeconomic, that it is not asked about specific advice that it has given to the President (and doesn't answer if it is), and that a somewhat special relationship is maintained with its political twin, the Joint Economic Committee. The reasons for these constraints are well known, and I will not labor them.

I have no idea what may have changed since my day in the Council's relationships with the Federal Reserve, although the Humphrey-Hawkins Act—with its at least implicit directive to the Federal Reserve to pursue the short-term economic goals established by the President—might suggest greater coordination of activities, both in determining and in pursuing the goals. However, given the traditional tenderness of the Federal Reserve about its internal affairs, and particularly about its relationships with the White House, it does not surprise me that little has been said publicly by either side about the details of the relationship.

With due apologies to Walter Heller, who coined the term, I always considered our talk about a "Quadriad" to have been rather exaggerated. At least through the 1960s, the relationship implied by that term did not seem to me to have much substance. In the late 1960s, to be sure, we finally established a certain amount of formal joint staff work between the Troika agencies and the Fed on policy matters; and we even produced some memoranda formally bearing the Fed chairman's signature along with those of the heads of the Troika agencies. I don't know what has happened since, but I would be interested to learn about the negotiations that preceded the imposition of credit controls last April as well as the monetary policy change of October 1979. To what extent and how were they cleared through the Economic Policy Group?

My own view has always been—and remains—that the almost complete independence of the Fed is unnecessary and undesirable. But I do not expect to live to see that independence seriously compromised. Thus the Council's relationships with the Fed are likely to remain both sensitive and often unsatisfactory.

The Economic Advisers
and the Economics Profession

In that fascinating interchange that Walter Heller arranged in December 1973 among then current and former Council members on the subject "How Political Must the Council of Economic Advisers Be?," Jim Tobin was asked about an economic adviser's responsibilities to the economics profession. He answered, essentially, that the adviser's responsibility was fulfilled by acting professionally. Herbert Stein added a responsibility for representing "the interests of the economics profession in the statistics that the government provides and in other government services useful for economics." I agree with both of these answers. Stein also referred to a responsibility "to be informed about the views of the profession and about what the profession knows and . . . to be able to make clear to the president what the range of professional opinion is." In the same exchange, Henry Wallich proposed the question, "What responsibility has the profession with respect to the Council?"—which no one tried to answer.

I do think that the relationship—in *both* directions—between the economic advisers in the government and the economics profession is an important matter, however amorphous. It is part of a larger question about the general relationship between the economics professional and public policy. And here, I guess, I must be somewhat critical of our profession.

My criticisms relate to what I see as: 1) a widespread retreat away from content and relevance in academic economics and into the investigation of puzzles that often seem to be selected mainly because they permit the use of ever more sophisticated mathematical techniques; 2) even when the names of the questions investigated bear some relationship to real-world policy problems, their substance is too often assumed away by the axioms of perfect knowledge, perfect foresight, perfect competition, and maximizing behavior that extends not over the business cycle, or even a lifetime, but over endless generations of descendants; 3) economic theorists who are openly contemptuous of their colleagues' "main-line" macroeconometric models nevertheless often assume that every economic actor has in his head (or available for inexpensive purchase) the numerical output (including measures of variance) of a very different, but equally complicated macromodel—which embodies everything that can be known about the "true" structure of the economy; 4) because they are unable to discern the economic efficiency or rationality of certain widespread forms of individual and institutional behavior, many economists argue that it is appropriate to build models that fail to incorporate these forms of behavior; 5) although they are often contemptuous of their colleagues who become seriously involved in providing advice to political leaders, some economists do not hesitate to offer their own half-baked policy advice, such as massive tax cuts that will immediately increase government revenues.

Clearly, our profession is providing divergent and confusing advice on economic policy. There is no way we could discipline the profession even if we wanted to, which we surely don't. And there are real and crucially important substantive disagreements. This situation makes it exceedingly difficult for the uninitiated to distinguish professionals from charlatans. Still, there are many matters on which, for example, Monetarists and Keynesians can agree. And we could have—and we need—more coherent and consistent government policies, whether all or even many economists would fully agree with their precise formulation. But this requires some willingness of members of our profession who are not in the government to be supportive of those who work as government advisers.

I may be greatly mistaken, but I believe that from perhaps the late 1950s through the mid-1970s the majority of our professional colleagues in the universities and research institutions, and even in private business, were on the whole sympathetic with and supportive of those who chose to work as economic advisers in government. I sense that this is not the case today. Yet it seems to me that public policy problems today are more complex, more difficult, and more dangerous for society than they were earlier. There is more, not less, need for economists to wrestle with these problems—in their own research, analysis, and teaching, and by serving as government economic advisors. Yet I see a retreat from admitting the existence of today's problems, from efforts to analyze them meaningfully, from willingness to serve in government or to give sympathetic support for those who do serve.

There are other changes even more important that have been creating difficulties for economic policy making: severe external shocks, usually of an inflationary character;

a further deterioration of an effective relationship between Congress and the President, perhaps mainly as the result of changes in the nature and operation of political parties; an exacerbation of conflict among social and political groups; and, I believe, increasing rigidities in the structure of economic organizations. There is little that professional economists can do about these changes other than to recognize their existence. But those advising and commenting from outside the government could be more supportive of those advising from within. And, perhaps, those advising from within should make more effort than they recently have to maintain contacts with the profession outside. It is at least possible that such a closer relationship could contribute to some redirection of the profession's interests and research toward a more meaningful analysis of the very real and critical problems of government economic policy in the 1980s.

Kennedy Economics Revisted

Walter W. Heller

Though much of the conference out of which this volume grew was devoted to a reappraisal of the economic experience of the 1960s, the major emphasis throughout was on its relevance to the unfolding experience of the 1980s. Rather than savoring the satisfactions of "the good old days," the participants treated the past as prologue.

What approaches to investment stimulus do the initiatives and experiences of the 1960s seem to validate? What do the 1960s have to offer the 1980s in the formulation and management of fiscal and monetary policy? Does the remarkable price stability of the early 1960s suggest that incomes policies have a logical role to play in trying to bring the inflation of the 1980s under control? Do the tax cuts of the 1960s, in fact, provide as much aid and comfort for "supply-side tax cuts" as their proponents claim?

The vigorous give-and-take of the conference on such questions as these reflected a first-hand knowledge of the economic events and policies of the 1960s by economists who had been "present at the creation." The passage of time and the sour economic experience of the 1970s have led to new perspectives and some sobering second thoughts. But the analysis and discussion were consistently anchored in a high-fidelity perception of the economic thinking, the economic policies, and the economic record of the 1960s. In sharp contrast, much of the recent discussion of that economic experience—and especially of the

1964 tax cut—seems strangely out of focus. Lessons are being drawn for which the actual experience of the 1960s provides little warrant.

The super-supply-siders, feverishly searching for historical reeds on which to lean, reinterpret the 1964 tax-cut experience as an undiluted supply-side success story. Many an anti-Keynesian, who comes not to praise but to bury the 1960s, sees only a total preoccupation with demand management, with fine tuning, and with "fiscalism."[1] And an occasional aberrant assures us that the expansion of the early 1960s traces almost entirely to a military buildup.

My endeavor in this brief commentary, as objectively as is possible for a direct participant in the process, is to put the experience of the early 1960s back into focus. In the process, I will try not to fall prey to the syndrome that "the past remembers better than it lived." I cannot claim complete objectivity, but I have at every possible point tested my recollection of events and policies and the thinking that lay behind them against not just the data but the public and private statements (as in our *Economic Reports*, speeches, testimony, and memoranda to the president) that we were making at the time. What emerges —or reemerges, since in part this is a repetition of oft-told tales—will, I hope, be useful in evaluating the views of the latter-day revisionists.

It may be worthwhile to start out by asking: What was so new about the "New Economics," as the press quickly dubbed the Economics of the New Frontier in 1961? Surely not the theory—much of that went back nearly a

---

1. This position, in extreme form, is typified by Irving Kristol (*Wall Street Journal*, December 19, 1980): "The Keynesian assumption was that, so long as total demand is adequate to achieve full employment, one need pay no attention to the incentives to save, invest, or engage in entrepreneurial risk-taking. Indeed, one could safely frustrate those incentives through taxation and regulation, just so long as our clever economists on the Council of Economic Advisers 'fine-tuned' economic demand to the proper level."

quarter of a century to John Maynard Keynes. What *was* new, however, was the translation of modern economics into practice—and into numerical targets—under the leadership of a willing and responsive president. At the very outset, President Kennedy directed his Council of Economic Advisers to "return not just to the letter but to the spirit of the Employment Act of 1946."

The Main Components

The distinctive stamp that the Kennedy administration put on economic policy and policymaking was made up of half a dozen major elements.

First, the ambiguous mandate of the Employment Act of 1946 to achieve "maximum employment, production, and purchasing power" was translated into the concrete goals of full employment, price stability, more rapid growth, and external payments equilibrium (under the constraints of maintaining freedom of economic choice and promoting greater equality of economic opportunity).

Second and perhaps more important, the Council converted the key qualitative goals into specific quantitative targets, and the President endorsed those targets. Thus in place of a general but vague commitment to "full employment," as in the Eisenhower years, the Kennedy administration adopted a specific target of 4-percent unemployment (at a time, by the way, when the 1960 recession had boosted unemployment to 7 percent). The target for economic growth—that is, the growth in the economy's potential to produce—was set at 4 percent per year in place of the 3 percent to 3-1/2 percent rate of growth in potential GNP in the 1953-60 period (and the 2-1/2 percent actual rate of expansion of real GNP in that period).

As to price stability, the goal was to maintain the very low rate of inflation of just over 1 percent per year that had been left as a welcome legacy of the Eisenhower era (at the heavy cost of three recessions in eight years, high unemployment, and low rates of growth). Once these numerical targets were adopted and accepted throughout government, they exerted a discipline on policy that the more abstract and qualitative goals could not achieve.

The third element was the concomitant shift in policy focus from moderating the swings of the business cycle to achieving the full-employment potential of the economy. It was not enough simply to reverse recessions and temper expansions. Success was to be measured in terms of hitting a moving target, namely, the rising full-employment potential of the economy. The point was to close the gap between actual and potential output without triggering inflation.

The concepts of full-employment potential and gap-closing were not brand new; they traced back to the bold and innovative Truman Council under the leadership of Leon Keyserling. But until Kennedy came along, the country never had a president who was willing to embrace such seemingly unorthodox doctrines and unabashedly move modern economics to the front burner.

Fourth was the development of a new policy of voluntary wage–price restraint. The Kennedy wage–price guideposts were introduced in January 1962 to induce labor and business to hold wage and price increases within the bounds of productivity advances and thus help ensure that fiscal-monetary stimulus would not run off into higher prices and wages but would instead express itself in higher output, jobs, profits, and investment. Indeed, the 1961–65 record strongly suggests that the guideposts played their part; wage increases in manufacturing did stay within the bounds of productivity increases, thus contributing to continued price stability and a sustained advance in real wages and living standards. Corporate profits doubled in those years.

Fifth, less tangible but no less important, was the orchestration of policy through skilled White House management utilizing such instruments as the Troika (the heads of Treasury, Budget, and CEA) and the Quadriad (adding in the Federal Reserve chairman). Economic policy differences were ironed out and presented to Congress and the public as a united and coherent effort. The vital ingredient in this was the leadership by a sagacious president, quick to accept modern economic thinking and to reject the old clichés that had hobbled policy. Banished were the beliefs that deficits in a weak economy were instruments of the devil and that public debt was a "burden on our grandchildren." John F. Kennedy was the first president to set aside these shibboleths, to fix budget balance not every year but at full employment as his target, and thus to facilitate a more activist economic policy.

A counterpart of the new activism was the president's use of the White House "as a pulpit for public education in economics" (a use he urged on us even before his inauguration). Just as he constantly urged his staff to explain and clarify national economic goals, concepts, and policies to the press, on television, and so on, the president himself provided a sense of direction through his own speeches to business and financial groups, national television programs, press conferences, and the famous Yale speech in June of 1962.

Finally, one should mention the quality of economic thinking that President Kennedy attracted throughout his administration. Outside the CEA, it was typified in the outstanding economic and fiscal leadership of David Bell in the budget bureau, Douglas Dillon and Robert Roosa in the Treasury, George Ball in the State Department, and

Carl Kaysen in the White House. The CEA had as council
members Kermit Gordon, James Tobin, Gardner Ackley,
and John Lewis; as staff members, people like Kenneth
Arrow, William Capron, Richard Cooper, Arthur Okun,
George Perry, Vernon Ruttan, Norman J. Simler, Warren
Smith, Robert Solow, Nancy Teeters, and Lloyd Ulman;
and as close-in consultants, the likes of Otto Eckstein,
John Meyer, Joseph Pechman, Paul Samuelson, and
Charles Schultze.

The First Year: Supply-Side Economics

Except for a quick but mild dose of demand stimulus in
an early 1961 antirecession package, the first year was
essentially a year of supply- and cost-side measures. We did
not use the catch phrase, "supply-side economics," but
that's exactly what it was. The actions speak for
themselves:

- Introduction of the investment credit, to this day the
  backbone of tax incentives for growth through business capital formation. Proposed in 1961, it was not
  enacted until 1962, largely because of misgivings and
  often hostility of both the business and labor communities. (Either because of its novelty or because of
  its form, the investment tax credit was at first opposed by many business leaders. Secretary Douglas
  Dillon was fond of telling the story of a business
  leader who asked him to explain it, step by step, and
  at the end added, "One last question: Why am I
  against it?".)
- Liberalization of tax depreciation guidelines, also put
  into effect in 1962.
- The "monetary twist," designed to reduce long-term
  interest rates and make more funds available for

long-term investment while holding up short-term
rates to cut international outflows of funds.

- Stepped-up investment in human capital through
worker training and retraining programs.

- The use of wage–price guideposts to help ensure that
stimulative measures would not run off into wage and
price inflation.

- Perhaps least well recognized, the decision in late
1961 to go for the "Cambridge–New Haven Growth
School" formula of tilting the fiscal-monetary mix to
favor capital formation relative to consumption.
How? By holding off on tax cuts in the hope that the
economy could struggle up to full employment under
the then-existing burden of taxation and thus produce a full-employment surplus. This would increase
saving and facilitate investment.

Let me pause here to note two oft-misunderstood points.
The first is that while the supply-side effects of tax cuts
on work effort and on saving are murky at best, there's no
doubt that running a surplus at full employment would
have positive supply-side effects. To be more specific:

- True, the bulk of the evidence does show a significant
investment response to sharply targeted measures like
investment tax credits and more liberal depreciation.

- But on work response, the evidence is ambiguous.
Countless studies show that existing workers' responses to tax cuts are an amalgam of: 1) added work
by some—the "eager beavers"—as they keep a larger
proportion of their rewards for work effort and thus
see the cost of leisure going up; 2) no change by
those who are locked into a pattern of fixed hours;
and 3) reduced work by those "laid-back" members of the labor force who ease off because they
can now achieve their income-after-tax targets with
fewer hours of work. Contrary to loose – but

ever-confident—assertions by some supply-side economists, painstaking research has not yet established for
sure even the sign, plus or minus, of workers' net
response, let alone the magnitude. (Studies do show
that increases in take-home pay elicit significant positive responses of labor effort by spouses and other
second earners.)

- Similarly, on savings, we are not quite sure which
  response dominates: to save *more* in the light of
  lower taxes on savings or to save *less* since lower
  taxes enable the saver to achieve a given target living
  standard with less saving. However, most economists
  agree that, on net balance, there is a positive response
  of saving to tax cuts.

- We do know that when governments cut their deficits
  or run surpluses, *that* constitutes net saving (i.e.,
  either reduced dissaving or positive saving) and re-
  leases funds for business investment and housing,
  provided that the economy is not operating at low
  ebb and that the monetary authorities do not offset
  the effect by single-minded pursuit of the wrong
  target.

The second point is that although President Kennedy
sought some significant expenditure increases from Congress, both for social programs and defense, his success
ratio on civilian programs was not high, and total defense
spending as a percentage of GNP declined steadily during
his administration.

I underscore the latter point because the idea that he got
the economy moving again through a defense buildup is a
canard that dies mighty hard. Recently, a *New York Times*
guest columnist confidently asserted that "the higher
growth rates of the 1960s were achieved only after President Kennedy succeeded in persuading Congress that, in
light of the Berlin crisis, defense spending should be

increased by 50 percent." In *absolute* terms, national defense expenditures rose less than 10 percent in the early 1960s, from $46 billion in 1960 to $50 billion by 1965. More important, in *relative* terms, defense outlays actually fell as a percentage of GNP, from 9 percent in 1960 to about 7-1/2 percent in 1965, just before escalation in Vietnam. So much for the notion that defense powered the 1961–65 expansion.

The Demand-Side Follow-Through: The 1965 Tax Cut

The shift to demand-side economics came in 1962 when it became painfully apparent that the overburden of taxes was so heavy that the economy could not achieve prosperity under its yoke. Alas, the Cambridge–New Haven hope for big full-employment surpluses had to go by the boards. With economic expansion faltering in 1962, with Congress in no mood to provide economic stimulus from the budget-spending side, and with top individual income tax rates still at 91 percent—far too high—we launched the offensive for a big tax cut in March of 1962. Its main purpose was to step up the pace of expansion and bring the economy up to its full-employment potential.

From March 1962 on, the Council campaigned for a $10 billion—later a $12 billion—tax cut. The Treasury was initially willing to go along with $3 or $4 billion of it, mainly to facilitate tax reform. But it was not until we hammered out an agreement in the Cabinet Committee on Growth late in 1962 that the President adopted the $12 billion tax-cut goal.

The tax cut's nine-month White House gestation period was then followed by 15 months of labor in Congress. To be pushing a large tax cut in the face of a sizable deficit and a rising economy was unprecedented. It was a rocky road. I remember all too vividly in early 1963 when Representative Martha Griffiths asked me, at a Joint Economic Committee hearing, why the American people were so loath to accept a tax cut. After I suggested that it might just be their puritan ethic, Representative John Byrnes of Wisconsin let me have it: "I'd rather be a puritan than a Heller."

Fairly early in the game, the President had to drop much of his reform package in order to clear the track for the cut itself. And much of the Kennedy cabinet voiced only lukewarm support (and some, privately, opposition or apprehension) lest the tax cut deprive them of revenues needed for their programs. That it would stimulate the economy and provide a sounder basis for later increased appropriations was not an easy case to sell.

That calls for another word about the bizarre notion that a tax cut will pay for itself by so stimulating *supply*—by unleashing such torrents of work effort, savings, and investment—that the reflow of tax revenues will match the initail tax loss. When an economy is operating far below its potential, as in the early 1960s, a tax cut's *demand*-side effect boosts purchasing power and puts both idle machines and factories and idle workers back to work and thus broadens the tax base—not enough fully to pay for itself, but enough to cut the revenue loss significantly.[2]

The notion that a tax cut's prompt demand stimulus—let alone its long-delayed supply stimulus—could generate enough revenue to pay for itself is unfortunately not sup-

2. "Measuring the Impact of the 1964 Tax Reduction," in *Perspectives on Economic Growth*, W. W. Heller, ed. (New York: Random House, 1968).

ported by either statistical evidence or cold analysis.[3] (One time, in an exuberant response to a leading question by the late Senator Hubert Humphrey, then chairman of the Joint Economic Committee, I suggested that the tax cut had paid for itself—but on careful inspection of the evidence, I publicly recanted later in a letter to the *Wall Street Journal*.)

In any event, the tax cut—20 percent for individuals and, in combination with the earlier tax breaks for business, 20 percent for corporations—became law after President Kennedy's death. To a remarkable degree, it "delivered the goods" until it was overtaken by Vietnam events:

- Enacted in March 1964, it stimulated a more vigorous expansion of the economy and reduction of unemployment without agitating inflation. The specific numbers: by July of 1965 (just before escalation of the war in Vietnam), the unemployment rate had dropped to 4.4 percent, while the consumer price index was rising at a rate of only 1.5 percent per year.

- Given the noninflationary environment, it was possible to put expansionary fiscal policy in harness with an accommodative monetary policy rather than having them pull in opposite directions.

---

3. A careful analysis by the Congressional Budget Office (in *An Analysis of the Roth-Kemp Tax Cut Proposal*, October 1978) reached the following conclusion:

"None of the models used by CBO showed that the increased economic activity generated by the tax cut raised revenues and lowered counter-cyclical transfer payments enough to make the tax rate reductions self-financing. Instead, the models showed a net increase in the federal deficit, after three years, of $5 billion to $13 billion above the level in the no-tax-cut simulations. Although the estimates made by others also show considerable variation, CBO is unaware of any systematic study of the 1964 tax cut that indicates that is was self-financing." (Page 38)

Further analysis of feedback effects of tax cuts was contained in the CBO study, *Understanding Fiscal Policy*, Background paper (April 1978), pp. 23–25.

- Dropping top individual tax rates from 91 percent to 70 percent helped to weaken somewhat the incentives for tax avoidance and strengthen the incentives for investment, while easing of low-bracket rates and tightening of the capital gains tax helped improve the equity of the tax structure.

- In a two-track policy, emphasizing both demand and supply stimulus, the tax cuts provided a powerful boost to demand while at the same time providing strong incentives to increase risk-taking and enlarge the flow of investment funds. In point of fact, the ratio of private investment to GNP reached a new postwar peak in 1965. (Yet, one cannot simply equate added investment with faster productivity growth, as demonstrated by the simultaneous slowdown of productivity growth and step-up of capital accumulation after the 1964 tax cut).

- As later events proved, the surest path to more adequate financing for government programs was, paradoxically, through tax reduction. With the acceleration of expansion through the tax cut, the economy soon returned to full prosperity. Both the atmosphere thus created and the resulting generous flows of federal, state, and local revenues led the country to a more sympathetic attitude toward expansion of government social programs. As President Kennedy put it in a conversation just eleven days before his death, "First we'll get your tax cut, and then we'll get my expenditure programs." And on November 19, he assured me that a direct attack on poverty would be part of his 1964 program. The 17 percent rise in GNP in the two years after the tax cut—between the first quarters of 1964 and 1966—made possible a 13-1/2 percent rise in government spending at lower average tax rates.

The tax cut proved the flip side of the Kennedy dictum that success has a thousand fathers, but failure is an orphan. In a perverse way, I treasure an April 1964 release by the American Taxpayers Union of New Jersey assuring one and all that it had "planned, initiated, and spearheaded the crusade that resulted in the recent [federal] tax cut." Showing a nice sense of proportion, it went on to note its support of legalized off-track betting.

Successful as the tax cut was, one has to add one disappointing postscript. When, with Vietnam, the time came for President Johnson and the Congress to turn the "New Economics" around—to use tax increases to cut aggregate demand and subdue inflation—the political process was found wanting. It was not until mid-1968 that a tax increase was finally enacted. Meanwhile, the superimposing of some $25 billion per year of Vietnam expenditures on an economy already programmed for full employment had done its malevolent work, overheating the economy and letting the inflationary tiger out of its cage.

Against the great human and political tragedy of Vietnam, the economic cost may not loom so large. But without that tragic war, I doubt very much that we would have been blown so far off the course of economic-growth-with-price-stability on which President Kennedy set us in his exhilarating thousand days.

Conference Participants
(with affiliations at time of conference)

Gardner Ackley
University of Michigan

Dwayne Andreas
Archer Daniels Midland Company

Kenneth J. Arrow
Stanford University

Atherton Bean
Minneapolis, Minnesota

Roy Blough
Silver Spring, Maryland

Francis M. Boddy
University of Minnesota

Barry P. Bosworth
The Brookings Institution

E. Cary Brown
Massachusetts Institute of Technology

O. H. Brownlee
University of Minnesota

John S. Chipman
University of Minnesota

Edward Coen
University of Minnesota

Richard N. Cooper
U.S. Department of State

Bruce B. Dayton
Wayzata, Minnesota

Frederick L. Deming
National City Bancorporation

Edward F. Denison
U.S. Department of Commerce

L. Laslo Ecker-Racz
Arlington, Virginia

Otto Eckstein
Harvard University

Roger D. Feldman
University of Minnesota

Edward M. Foster
University of Minnesota

Richard Goode
International Monetary Fund

Walter P. Heller
University of California, San Diego

Walter W. Heller
University of Minnesota

James M. Henderson
University of Minnesota

Lawrence Hickey
Stein Roe and Farnham

Clifford Hildreth
University of Minnesota

Charles A. Holt
University of Minnesota

Leonid Hurwicz
University of Minnesota

Takatoshi Ito
University of Minnesota

C. Bernard Jacobs
National City Bank of Minneapolis

James S. Jordan
University of Minnesota

John H. Kareken
University of Minnesota

Stephen F. Keating
Honeywell, Inc.

Anne O. Krueger
University of Minnesota

Donald S. Lamm
W. W. Norton and Company

Robert Lampman
University of Wisconsin

David M. Lilly
University of Minnesota

Jon Lovelace
Capital Research and Management Company

Franco Modigliani
Massachusetts Institute of Technology

Herbert Mohring
University of Minnesota

Richard A. Musgrave
Harvard University

Robert R. Nathan
Robert R. Nathan Associates

William C. Norris
Control Data Corporation

John E. Pearson
Northwestern National Life Insurance Company

Joseph A. Pechman
The Brookings Institution

George L. Perry
The Brookings Institution

William G. Phillips
International Multifoods

John S. Pillsbury, Jr.
Northwestern National Life Insurance Company

Robert Porter
University of Minnesota

Marcel K. Richter
University of Minnesota

Alice M. Rivlin
Congressional Budget Office

Marshall A. Robinson
The Russell Sage Foundation

Mark S. Rosenzweig
University of Minnesota

Vernon W. Ruttan
University of Minnesota

Walter S. Salant
The Brookings Institution

Paul A. Samuelson
Massachusetts Institute of Technology

Thomas J. Sargent
University of Minnesota

G. Edward Schuh
University of Minnesota

Charles L. Schultze
President's Council of Economic Advisers

Louis Shere
Bloomington, Indiana

Leonard Silk
The New York Times

N. J. Simler
University of Minnesota

Christopher A. Sims
University of Minnesota

Joel Slemrod
University of Minnesota

Harlan M. Smith
University of Minnesota

Robert M. Solow
Massachusetts Institute of Technology

Craig E. Swan
University of Minnesota

James Tobin
Yale University

John G. Turnbull
University of Minnesota

Lloyd Ulman
University of California, Berkeley

Neil Wallace
University of Minnesota

Conference Sponsors

Andreas Foundation
Decatur, Illinois

Atherton Bean
Minneapolis, Minnesota

Capital Research and Management Company
Los Angeles, California

Control Data Corporation
Minneapolis, Minnesota

Dayton Hudson Foundation
Minneapolis, Minnesota

Honeywell, Inc.
Minneapolis, Minnesota

International Multifoods Corporation
Minneapolis, Minnesota

National City Bank of Minneapolis
Minneapolis, Minnesota

Northwestern National Life Insurance Company
Minneapolis, Minnesota

Joseph Rosenfield
Des Moines, Iowa

Stein Roe and Farnham
Chicago, Illinois